Tynwald (I)

Ben-my-Chree (II)

Viking

King Orry (III)

Mona's Isle (VI)

ISLAND LIFELINE

Manxman and *Mona's Isle*.
Reproduced by courtesy of *Ships Monthly*
from a painting by John Nicholson.

ISLAND LIFELINE

Connery Chappell

81 20752

19 80

T. STEPHENSON & SONS LTD.
PRESCOT : MERSEYSIDE

ISBN 0 901314 20 X

√

Printed and made in Great Britain by
T. Stephenson & Sons Ltd., Prescot, Merseyside.

To my wife
Joan
for her wit and wisdom
in this and many other
collaborations

Contents

List of Illustrations

CHAPTER FOUR

CHAPTER FIVE

CHAPTER SIX

CHAPTER SEVEN

CHAPTER EIGHT

CHAPTER NINE
(all photographs taken aboard *Lady of Mann* (II))

CHAPTER TEN

CHAPTER ELEVEN

CHAPTER TWELVE

CHAPTER THIRTEEN

Foreword

It is my good fortune to be the Chairman of the Steam Packet Company as we approach its one hundred and fiftieth anniversary, still operating independently, still with the same, well-known title, still free from amalgamation or take-over.

Such an occasion in the Company's life calls for recognition and for its history to be recorded and brought up-to-date. In this respect we have been fortunate in finding on the island a writer of the calibre of Mr. Connery Chappell, who has devoted much time and energy in delving into the records of the Company from the very beginnings in the 1830s down to the present time. Much interesting information has been unearthed, particularly regarding the early days. The result is an absorbing and comprehensive story, which, together with the numerous illustrations, provides a book which must deservedly appeal to a wide readership, not only among Manxmen but among shiplovers all over the world.

T. E. Brownsdon.

The
ISLE OF MAN
STEAM PACKET
CO. LTD.

QUOCUNQUE JECERIS STABIT

CHAPTER ONE: *Origins*

THE ISLE OF MAN STEAM PACKET COMPANY has a fair claim to the right to call itself the oldest surviving shipping line in the coastal division of the British merchant fleet. It is certainly a honour no Manxman would dispute, for the company was formed in 1830 and adopted its present name in 1832. It was by no means the first in the long list of British shippers but few of the other pioneers have survived or managed to preserve their original identity into modern times. There were many failures on the way and the take-over bids and amalgamations of recent years have removed the remainder of the names.

Burns and Laird of London was founded back in 1814 but it is now part of the vast P. & O. group; Clyde Shipping, formed in 1815, is now a unit in F. T. Everard. General Steam Navigation, established in 1824, was a most famous name in shipping history but its identity is now lost by its absorption into P. & O. The same thing happened to the Belfast Steamship Company, which started operations in 1825. The P. & O. itself evolved in 1837 from the Peninsular Line, which had been formally founded in 1834. Indeed, of the entire British merchant fleet, Bibby seems to be the only surviving name that is even older than the Manx company.

The Steam Packet Company remains independent and the three-legged symbol of the Isle of Man, painted on the paddle boxes of its first vessel, has now been carried on its ships for 150 years.

Long before 1830, however, there were sea links between England and the island. The Manx are by tradition a maritime people. Back in the eighteenth century they divided their working time between fishing, farming, mining and smuggling. In the last of these, their boats sailed far abroad, as had those of the Vikings in the same seas many centuries earlier. So considerable was the loss to the British revenue from contraband running in the Irish Sea that in 1765 the Crown purchased the strategically placed Isle of Man from the Atholl family, and the Redcoats moved in. The Manx liked it not. Two years later, perhaps with the intention of throwing a helping line to their garrison on the island, Westminister organised a weekly packet boat service between Douglas and Whitehaven.

That was the start. The crossing could be terrible; it was not unknown for boats to be driven back to Cumberland after days at sea. There were times in the winter when the island was cut off for weeks on end. Yet despite the harshness and unreliability of the sea crossing the population increased steadily, even though its poverty could at times be desperate. Too many of its young men left, anxious to escape the penury of the thin soil; they wanted something more promising than the often hazardous fishing and the hard life of the mines. But the human traffic was two-way; the packet boat brought people from the mainland, some adventurous and wanting change, some merely escaping creditors, for debts incurred in the United Kingdom could not be enforced on the Isle of Man. The island's population even doubled between 1767, when the first regular sailings were started, and 1829, increasing from 20,000 to 40,000. The Manx may have been poor, but they tilled their soil, spoke their own tongue, and loved their island.

From the beginning of the 19th century many things happened to open up the island to an increasing amount of traffic. Work on the Red Pier at Douglas had commenced in 1793 and was completed in 1801. By then the sides of the small Douglas River basin had been shorn up and an attempt had been made to push some sort of protective structure out to sea. It had failed. Back in 1787 the first pier had given up the struggle against the winter storms and had become a shelf of rubble under the waves. So for years the Douglas harbour was fully exposed to the easterly gales; in the Bay the perilous Conister Rock claimed many victims. The Red

Douglas Harbour about the middle of the last century.

Pier, built from the pocket of the British Treasury, cost £25,000. It was driven out to the limit of low water, and went more than 50 yards beyond the end of the old wrecked pier that had preceeded it.

Even so, for 70 years until 1871, passengers had to board rowing boats from the pier and be helped aboard any vessel lying off. The reverse applied when they were disembarking. The scene could be chaotic and blasphemous and in the winter the weary passenger would step ashore wet and exhausted.

In 1815 sail was giving way to engine. The first steamer called at the island on its voyage from the Clyde to Liverpool, and in 1819 James Little opened the first steamship service to the island, using it as a port of call between Liverpool and Greenock. A year later his service was augmented, with three ships appearing on the station. In announcing the sailings of the *Majestic* and the *City of Glasgow* agent James Little of Greenock was able to say proudly that the full journey from the Clyde to the Mersey was 'usually' made within 25 hours. These two vessels, he claimed, each with one tall chimney stack and three sailing masts, with the Royal Arms engraved on the paddle boxes, carried no goods but were fitted up for the comfort of the passengers; the first class fare was 17s. 6d. from the Isle of Man to Liverpool, a price that included provisions and steward's fees; second class was without provisions and cost 9s. 6d. A coach could be carried on deck for £4. 15s., and a pair of dogs for 10s. Passengers were put on board and landed free of charge.

The journey between Douglas and Liverpool at first took about 10 hours, later usually reduced to nine. It was a seasonal trade; there were no winter services.

James Little soon met competition. The thrustful St. George Steam Packet Company of Liverpool started a service between Liverpool and Glasgow in 1822, using the *St. George*, an outstanding ship of its day. It called at Douglas. Within a few years the traffic between Liverpool and the Clyde grew to such an extent that the New Clyde Shipping Company, the Royal Mail and the steam packets of the War Office were all engaged in the trade and calling at Douglas on the journey.

During this surge of activity a small steamer, the *Triton*, was put on mail service between Whitehaven and the island, sailing during the winter. This tiny 30 ton vessel had been built in Bordeaux and had plied between Le Havre and Rouen making three round trips each week. It came into the Manx service in 1826, crossing from the mainland once a week, and the island was at last getting some sort of service all through the year, always providing that the weather was fair.

It was plainly not yet good enough. The Manx had their national pride and the seafaring tradition of the island meant much to them. It was essential that they should have their own service.

Such was the feeling that in 1826 a Manxman named Cosnahan, living in Liverpool, took over a new steamer, the *Victory*, put her on the Douglas run for two months and then offered to syndicate shares in his enterprise. His proposition was for the Manx public to take shares of £50, with a free passage for anyone who took three shares or more. He called a meeting in Douglas in November, 1826, but failed to get the support he had expected. He may have been surprised and disappointed, for Cosnahan was an old and respected Manx name. The family was said to have been founded by a vicar of Santon and to have produced a number of Manx lawyers and clerics.

Cosnahan continued his efforts; the *Victory* remained on its weekly run for the rest of the winter, and did three round trips a week during the early part of the summer of 1827. Then this small vessel, of a mere 36 h.p. and 112 tons, was purchased by Ross for one of his expeditions in search of the elusive North West Passage. She was abandoned in the Arctic two years later. Although the *Victory* had been of some transitory help to them, the Manx continued to feel a grievance. The winter service to the mainland was pitiful and unreliable; the lack of comfort was deplorable. The going could be hard and tardy. There was too much dependence on wind and weather in the sailing schedules.

For sixty years, as one writer said, the accommodation had remained just as miserable, despite the change from sail to steam.

At the end of 1829 the move forward was finally taken. The meeting that was to result in the formation of the island's own steam packet company was presided over by James Quirk, High Bailiff of Douglas. The date was December 17. The discussion was exploratory and not a lot is known about it. According to one source it was held at the Court House, but this was not so. The meeting was at the Dixon and Steele sale rooms down by Douglas harbour.

Rather more than 50 years later a woman wrote and published a genteel booklet in which she revealed the full horrors she had experienced on an early steamer crossing and claimed that her sufferings resulted in the formation of the Isle of Man Steam Packet Company. This 'Widow Lady', as she called herself, told how all those years ago she had crossed to the island from Liverpool in a small steamer called the *Alice* which was carrying the mail while the Glasgow packet was under repair. The crossing was very rough and she became ill. On going down to the cabin she found that there were no sofas and no berths and only a bare table in the centre of the room. She was laid down on the floor with a sailor's jacket as a pillow, and covered with a tarpaulin. No tea was available but she was given a little brandy and water and fell asleep. The reader might feel that this was only to be expected when a fastidious lady met with a little brandy under such rude conditions. However, news of her horrid journey, she alleged, spread around when she was landed, and writing after an interval of more than 50 years she claimed that two gentlemen called on her, listened aghast to her report of the nightmare crossing, rose in their wrath and called a meeting at the Court House from which the Steam Packet Company resulted.

There may have been some substance to most of her story, but it is more likely that the Manx did not like the domination of the St. George Company. It had been awarded the mail contract in 1828. This meant that Whitehaven was no longer the vital link with the island and Liverpool was substituted, and with the small *Triton* now out of service the St. George directors had too large a say in island affairs. Yet they made the mistake of maintaining their winter service only once weekly, using small and slow ships with no cover or amenities for passengers. To the Manx enough was more than enough. It was too much.

The meeting in the Douglas sale rooms followed. No record was taken, but a committee was appointed to 'ascertain the cost of a steam packet'. It was decided to form a new company and £4,500 was at once subscribed from the floor. Resolute holders of familiar Manx names were present; Quiggin, Moore, Gawne and Crebbin among others. Those who were not Manx included W. Wood of Glasgow, who was almost certainly a member of the family of John Wood, who had built the first British steamer, the *Comet*, back in 1812.

As weeks passed inquiries were made, the project progressed, and more meetings were held; a total of £7,250 was put up in 290 shares of £25 apiece.

The subscribers were astute. They knew who to lobby for future power. A deputation called on Lord Strathallan and pursuaded him to try to get the mail contract diverted to the new enterprise, at first called the Mona's Isle Company. It waited on Sir John Tobin and on General Goldie, major powers both on the small island, and as its completion neared the Company decided to name the first of its steamers the *Mona's Isle*.

It was launched on June 30th, 1830, having cost £7,052. The committee had succeeded where Cosnahan had so recently failed. They had established a truly Manx link between the island and the mainland. The Manx were satisfied.

CHAPTER TWO: *Rivals*

THE MONA'S ISLE COMPANY WAS IMMEDIATELY involved in determined and sometimes hazardous rivalry. In time the hazards vanished; under various house flags the competition was to appear and reappear across the next 150 years.

Not surprisingly, for William Wood of the shipbuilding family had attended that founders' meeting in Douglas and had been an original subscriber, the order for the first steamer went to the John Wood yard at Port Glasgow. Its engine was by Robert Napier, who was to become a distinguished name in the shipping world. Years later Napier stated that his reputation had been largely founded by the attention drawn to him by the success of the *Mona's Isle*. The ship was widely acclaimed and was fast for its day.

It was this speed factor that made the vessel so much talked about and helped to give the company a firm and successful basis. Yet it was the small ship's deck design and furnishings that first attracted the passengers, for she had ample undercover accommodation including berths.

The Manx public immediately decided that she was infinitely superior to the two vessels the St. George Company kept on the winter station. These were slower and uncomfortable, with no real provision for passengers and no shelter. Great therefore was the rejoicing among the Manx when they saw the island's three-legged symbol on the superior vessel.

On Monday, August 16, 1830, less than seven weeks after being launched in Scotland, the *Mona's Isle* made her first trip from Douglas to Liverpool. She carried fifteen saloon and seventeen steerage passengers, all of them with their berths allotted. So started the bitter competition with the St. George Company, whose *Sophia Jane* cast off from Douglas at the same time and arrived in Liverpool two minutes ahead. She was also first home on the return trip.

Never again was the *Mona's Isle* beaten. Two days later the Manx ship had asserted herself, coming in from Liverpool 40 minutes ahead of her rival. This business of racing the two ships, starting off from the same port at the same time, seems to verge on the crazy. It did not improve the service: it split it; far more sensible to have put the vessels on opposite stations and to have had them cross in mid-voyage. But at least the watchful public had a free entertainment.

The tale of this early rivalry has often been told. Its leading man was William Gill, a truly remarkable sea captain. After he had retired in 1852 the people of Liverpool gave him a handsome subscription including a gift of silver for his skill in discovering and opening the Victoria Channel into the Mersey, saving hours of delay entering the port. He had probed the Channel through the sands when in command of the *Mona's Isle* 20 years earlier. It had been a painstaking and outstanding exercise in seamanship.

Gill was born in 1795, in Glen Auldyn, outside the northern Manx town of Ramsey. The Glen marks a small and stoney watercourse that winds down from the northern end of the

5

island's central spine, and skirts Sky Hill, where the last battle was fought on Manx soil. In Gill's boyhood it ended in a few scattered farm cottages, whose occupants lived off the grazing land that rose from the coastal plain.

Gill is said to have been trained as a ship's carpenter, and may have worked at Ramsey's small shipyard, but he seems to have gone to sea while still a lad. Before he joined what is now the Steam Packet Company he rose to command in turn both the *Duchess of Athol* and the *Douglas*, sailing vessels that traded between Douglas and Liverpool.

It was originally intended by the Mona's Isle Company that Robert Crawford, a captain of a small steamer that traded on the Liverpool to Glasgow run, should be master of the first ship. Terms were agreed, but Crawford never started with the new line. Instead, Gill was selected. The choice was fortunate.

For Gill soon managed to show the stern to the *Sophia Jane*. His ship was new and had few sea hours behind it; a celebration trip to Menai Bridge for the enjoyment of the owners, taken only two days before the maiden voyage, was hardly enough to run in Napier's engine. However, once the *Mona's Isle* had settled down Gill established a normal schedule of $8\frac{1}{2}$ knots and an 8-hour crossing. In bad weather the difference between the crossing times of the rivals became even more marked. Given a gale, Gill was known to arrive winner by a full three hours, to the relief of his passengers. Such superiority was something of a triumph for the Manx company and there was much enthusiasm on the island. Souvenirs were produced in honour of the small vessel.

The St. George Company struck back. They started a price cutting war. Then in barely a month they withdrew the *Sophia Jane* and put on the *St. George*, their fastest and largest steamer. This gave Gill an opportunity to hit the opposition and hit it hard. He was lucky. For some weeks there had been this extraordinary timetable whereby the rival vessels had left port together; thus the humiliation of Lieutenant Tudor, the R.N. officer who commanded the *Sophia Jane*.

On the first night before the *St. George* and the *Mona's Isle* were due to leave Liverpool together, the very astute Gill looked at the sky and decided that a south-westerly gale was imminent. This would mean that the port paddlebox would take the full force of the wind and on the roll in the beam sea it could be thrashing the air. Gill met what he was sure was a pending emergency. He worked with his crew through the night, shifting coal and such other weight as there was to the windward. The *Mona's Isle* might then have a list to port in the Mersey, but once in the open sea she would settle on as even keel as could be expected in a strong south-west wind. The decision was a good one. Gill was first home with three hours to spare.

His skill and foresight had dramatic consequences late in November of that year. He had crossed to Douglas, watched his passengers go ashore, and realised that a south-easterly gale was blowing up. He decided to put to sea immediately; he then rode out the storm in safety far off-shore. Of all the winds that could pound the island the south-easterly was by far the most dangerous in Douglas Bay.

Lieutenant Tudor on the *St. George* took a different decision with appalling consequences. He decided to anchor in the Bay. His vessel broke its cable in the tempestuous night and the *St. George* ended pounded against the Conister Rock where she broke up. William Hillary, who was to found what eventually became the Royal National Lifeboat Institution, watched the proceedings from his post at the top of his home, Fort Anne, high up over what is now Douglas Harbour. Despite the gale he rowed out with volunteers and saved the ship's crew. Within two years he had built the Tower of Refuge, now a landmark for tourists, on the rock in the Bay.

The loss of their best vessel was a serious blow to the St. George Company. They persevered with the Douglas run for a few more months, but finally withdrew in June 1831. The *Mona's Isle* was left in possession of the field. It was the Manx company's first but most spectacular victory. The mail contract inevitably followed. The post was to be carried twice weekly in summer and once a week in the winter, and the contract with the Postmaster General was worth £1,000 a year, a goodly subsidy in those days.

The Manx directors were now proud and ambitious. It was obvious to them that the *Mona's Isle* was too prestigious and valuable a property for the once weekly winter run. A second vessel was ordered, from the John Wood yard. The *Mona* was the result. There was now the beginnings of a fleet.

Certainly the directors of the pioneer company were determined men. They worked with remarkable diligence. They met frequently but at irregular intervals; they reviewed the day to day affairs of the company and decided small matters that would now be left to department heads. Yet remarkably the really major decisions that would now be the province of the board were merely taken as recommendations and then submitted to the next meeting of stock-holders for approval.

These six-monthly meetings of the subscribers would now be regarded as *ad hoc* meetings of shareholders with no legal standing. But 150 years ago there was no such thing as a public limited liability company; the stockholders were the owners in a more personal sense than the shareholder of today. It was their brass and they wanted the final word on what was done with it. They made sure they dictated events.

This pattern went on for many years; no ship could be named without the approval of the stockholders; the very permission to build was held up until the main body of the company agreed. There was a simple reason for this dictatorship by the subscribers, although it slowly declined as the years advanced, and as the number of shares increased. The company had been formed on a basis of subscription units of £25, and these sufficed to pay for the *Mona's Isle*, the first vessel. Running expenses were defrayed from earnings but funds did not accumulate fast enough to pay for subsequent ships. Subscribers were thus invited to take up more and more stock, first in half units of £12.10s. Later even quarter units were accepted and outsiders invited to subscribe. In this way the company could fund its shipbuilding costs or meet the bank demands incurred for the same purpose.

Soon after Gill's victory over the *St. George* the directors at one of their frequent meetings restored the fares on the *Mona's Isle* to an economic level; there was no longer a price cutting war; the first class cabin on the Liverpool run was increased from 7s. 6d. to 15s. and the steerage from 2s. 6d. to 5s. And within another month the formidable Gill had been docked £2 as he was held responsible for a deficiency in the steward's returns on his vessel.

A year later he was awarded a testimonial of £100 in recognition of his services as master of the *Mona's Isle* and he was soon ordered to represent the company's interests in the Glasgow yards at the building of their third ship. He was the favoured son. But the directors were disciplinarians. Three years later he was in serious trouble. In September, 1835, he refused to go to sea one day as his brother was dying. He was dismissed. The incident had important consequences.

The dismissal brought to a head the strange relationship between the directors and the shareholders with their dominating *ad hoc* meetings. The proprietors met especially to consider the Gill matter and resolved that the sea captain had not been dismissed and that he be 'requested' to take command of the company's third ship. On receiving this motion the directors declined to give any explanation for Gill's dismissal. The shareholders again met in a pique and passed another resolution, this time dismissing the directors for their 'injudicious management for the last two months'. Gill stayed on. So did most of the directors.

Those who remained busied themselves at what they considered their duties. They discharged the cook of the *Mona's Isle* when he had been caught smuggling. They ordered that no steward or stewardess should be employed until the candidate had provided a security bond in favour of the company. They spent time over the case of some boys who had passed a bladder of brandy from a dinghy to the *Mona's Isle*. These were mighty matters to a small group of men whose minute book shows them to have been fussy, even petty, sometimes cheese-paring, but always determined and, in their way, just.

With three vessels in the fleet the company was certainly in expansionist mood. In 1834 it opened a daily two-way traffic between Douglas and Liverpool, sailing from the island at 8.0 a.m. and from Liverpool at 10 a.m. There were no Sunday sailings, following a resolution passed in 1831.

The monopoly that the Steam Packet Company had enjoyed since it succeeded in removing the formidable St. George Company from the station in 1831 could not be expected to last. The row over Gill's dismissal and reinstatement had caused a sharp schism among the directors and even some shareholders. In consequence there had been a number of resignations; William Duff and T. Garrett, both of whom had been founder subscribers to the company, were among them. A rival company with these men as two of the first three directors, was set up; the Isle of Man and Liverpool Steam Navigation Company.

The new company was formed at the end of 1835 and immediately ordered a new vessel, the *Monarch*, to be built by Steele with engines by Caird, both of Greenock. It was to be a 300-tonner driven by 150 horsepower, slightly more powerful than the Steam Packet Company's latest vessel, *Queen of the Isle*.

Sailings started in August, 1836, with a chartered vessel, the *Clyde*, the *Monarch* not having arrived on schedule. The real test came a month later, after the *Monarch* had been delivered. There is no doubt but that at first she was faster than the *Queen of the Isle*, despite the considerable skill of Gill, who could reasonably be said to have known more about the intricacies of the stormy Liverpool run than any other of the coastal sea captains. The new company was able to boast of quicker crossings, and boast it certainly did. Its advertisements on the island were aggresive in the extreme.

The result was another extraordinary price-cutting war in which single fares at cabin (first class) rate were 2s. 6d. and steerage 1s. The *Monarch* was withdrawn from the station in the autumn but was restored to it the following summer. This time the *Queen of the Isle* was more frequently the faster vessel. Such competition could not last. The fares were plainly uneconomic. The Isle of Man and Liverpool Steam Navigation Company collapsed at the end of 1837 and with it the *Monarch* was sold and vanished from Manx waters.

With the failure of its second competitor the Steam Packet Company was left in command of its station for 50 years, with the exception of a minor flare of rivalry in 1853 and 1854. This came from a company in Ramsey and another in Castletown. Both tried to get a substantial share of the insular trade with Liverpool but the bulk of the freight continued through Douglas. There was also a service between Liverpool and Glasgow which sometimes put in at Douglas on the way. None of these enterprises was strictly a full competitor of the Steam Packet Company, but their presence resulted in yet another price cutting war from which the established company was again to come out the winner.

The Ramsey owners had even persuaded the esteemed Captain Gill to come out of his retirement and command their vessel, the *Manx Fairy*, on its first run from Liverpool to Douglas. She started from the Mersey at the same time as the Steam Packet Company's *Mona's Queen* and beat her to the Isle of Man by eight minutes. So the strange old practice of racing the ships was resumed. The Ramsey vessel did not always win, and the *Mona's Queen* seems to have had the edge. The *Manx Fairy* was a well-appointed vessel of 400 tons and 200 h.p. but she was expensive to run, had little cargo space, and her draught was too much for Manx waters. In

1857 she had the ill fortune to sink a Birkenhead ferry, costing the Ramsey company nearly £2,000. Financial troubles developed; she was not a commercial proposition and she was soon compulsorily sold for £7,000, less than half her original cost of £16,000.

The purchasers were a syndicate of business men in Ramsey and they continued to run the vessel for four more years. It was an uneven fight and strenuous efforts were made to sell the *Manx Fairy* to the Steam Packet Company, who refused her.

Eventually she was sold for £6,000 to Cunard, Wilson, in turn to be sold to shipowners in Sicily, where, it was thought, the three-legged symbol on her paddle boxes would be appropriate, for the Sicilians had a not dissimilar emblem.

If Ramsey could have its own vessel, then Castletown must obviously not be left behind. The island's southern town was in fact the government centre and as such drew the professional men of the island. True, it was losing out to Douglas in the commercial field, and the success of the Steam Packet Company obviously added to this, but it was still the capital.

Less than a year after the arrival of Ramsey's *Manx Fairy* Castletown saw the launching of its own *Ellan Vannin*, a vessel of 350 tons register and 100 horsepower, with the important advantage of drawing merely seven feet of water. Yet hers was a poor career; she could outspeed her rivals in a calm sea but she had little draught for cargo. At one time her owners were driven to sending her to Liverpool via Douglas carrying passengers for a shilling ticket. There was a limit to such price cutting. It was financially disastrous and it could not last.

A tangle of arrangements was made between the Ramsey and Castletown companies, both concerns uniting against the Steam Packet Company. But the problem was insoluble; by June, 1858, the *Ellan Vannin*'s owners finally sold her to Cunard, Wilson, for the modest sum of £4,070. The Liverpool firm was acting for the government of Sardinia who took her and renamed her the *Achimedes*. The Steam Packet Company was soon left alone in the field once more, except for the vessels on the Liverpool to Glasgow run which called at Douglas.

So the Steam Packet Company prospered, helped by the general development of the Isle of Man and by its own determination in beating off rivals on its main route. By the first year of the second half of the century it was carrying 48,000 passengers annually, a splendid total compared with the 20,000 in its earliest years. The island was becoming a holiday resort for the better-off people in the industrial north and of Scotland and — to a much lesser extent — of Ireland. The days of the universal holiday, when the spinners and the pitmen could take their ease, were still some years away. Wages were too low to allow such luxuries. But as living standards slowly rose so the number of passengers increased. True there were poor years when an industrial recession bit into spending power; however, the overall pattern of the graph was upward.

The calm was broken in 1887 when a serious rival appeared. The Isle of Man, Liverpool and Manchester Steam Ship Company, of Liverpool, was generally known as the Manx Line. From the Fairfield Shipbuilding Company it bought two ships that were fast and well equipped for their day, the *Prince of Wales* and the *Queen Victoria*. They were paddle steamers of rather more than 1500 tons and with a high turn of speed, scheduled to be 20½ knots; but it was reported that during her trials over the measured mile on the Clyde the *Prince of Wales* recorded 24.25 knots, while earlier the *Queen Victoria* ran from Greenock to Liverpool in less than nine and a half hours, averaging 22½ knots; this was the fastest run so far known between the two ports, and it was achieved in a rough sea.

When the new rivals went into the Douglas service the curious business of racing the route started once more. The newcomers were usually a full half-hour faster than the Steam Packet Company's best vessels. The *Prince of Wales* once achieved the remarkable feat of steaming from the Rock at Liverpool to Douglas Head in a minute under three hours. It was said that Fairfield's had built the *Queen Victoria* and her sister ship as a speculation, paying particular attention to the needs of the Liverpool - Douglas run, and feeling sure that the Steam Packet Company would be the buyers.

Eventually they were, but by a different method. This time it was the Steam Packet Company, unable for once to compete against speed, which adopted the price-cutting ploy and drove the opposition into losses. A return saloon ticket on the route went down from 10s. 6d. to 5s. A single for the fore-cabin was as cheap as 1s. 6d. Season tickets could be bought for two guineas for first-class and 25s. for steerage. In the midst of this fierce competition the Steam Packet Company even introduced a seasonal second daily service each way between Douglas and Liverpool.

It was a cut-throat business; the new Manx Line delayed reducing its own fares for as long as possible, but after a few months, in August, the newcomer was forced to follow. It continued to advertise a 3½-hour crossing but it was still only achieving a small share of the passenger traffic and this at a time when there was a most welcome increase in the number of holiday visitors.

Cuts of this severity could only mean losses. The Steam Packet Company failed marginally to break even both in 1887 and 1888. The Manx Line, however, lost £5,300 in its first year and £3,500 in its second, without allowing anything for depreciation of its two vessel fleet. The Steam Packet had the deeper roots and the longer purse; negotiations started at the end of what would normally have been a most successful tourist season.

On November 23, 1888, the junior line sold out and vanished. The Steam Packet Company added the *Prince of Wales* and the *Queen Victoria* to its growing fleet. They were the first two captures from a defeated rival. The pattern was to be repeated.

Yet another competitor had appeared in 1887, the Isle of Man Steam Navigation Company, generally called the Lancashire Line. It possessed but one ship, the *Lancashire Witch*, and it did not stay in business for long. It lasted only until May, 1888, when the mortgagees

Douglas Harbour a century ago. The vessels at the pier are *Snaefell* (II) and in the outside berth *Manxman* (I) (ex *Antrim* (I)) of the Barrow S.N. Co. which was taken over by the Midland Railway in 1907.

foreclosed. The steamer, which averaged four hours on the main run from Douglas, was sold to Australia.

For seven more years the Steam Packet Company was free of rivalry. Then came the Mutual Line of Manx Steamers, Ltd., which chartered a slow paddle ship, the *Lady Tyler*. The effort started in May, and ended in bankruptcy in July. The Manx public had little time for the elderly vessel, which they quickly nicknamed the 'Lazy Toiler'.

The next challenger was an adventurous Liverpool businessman named S. W. Higginbottom, a Member of Parliament, who was a colliery owner among other enterprises. From the City of Dublin Steam Packet he purchased the *Munster* and the *Leinster*, two 1700-ton paddle vessels built about 1860. They had come off the Holyhead-Kingstown run and were advertised to start on the route between Douglas and Liverpool.

They never did. The Steam Packet Company bought them and later sold them for scrap. They never joined the Manx fleet. The purchase and resale prevented an opposition service.

But Higginbottom remained ambitious. In 1899 he formed Liverpool and Douglas Steamers, Limited. He purchased a paddle steamer of 1885, the *Ireland*, of 2000 tons, said to be capable of doing the Douglas crossing in 3 hours 20 minutes. He advertised forcibly. His new company quickly purchased the *Calais/Douvres*, the *Normandy*, the *Brittany*, the *Lily* and the *Violet*. Of the five, the first three had been cross-Channel steamers serving the ports to the Continent. The *Normandy* and *Brittany*, which had been plying between Newhaven and Dieppe, were small and slow. The *Lily* and the *Voilet* had previously been used by the London and North Western Railway on the Holyhead to Dublin route. They were somewhat more suitable than the two cross-Channel steamers but they were outpaced by the Steam Packet Company's *Empress Queen*. The *Ireland*, despite the hopeful advertisements, was a disappointment. She was a slightly larger vessel than the *Empress Queen*, but she was slower. Although she was a fine, large vessel she was out of date. Higginbottom's only really successful purchase was the *Calais/Douvres*, which had been built for the cross-Channel trade of the South Eastern and Chatham Railway by Fairfields of Govan, and although described as doing 18½ knots she had exceeded 22 on the Channel.

The upshot was yet another price-cutting war. First class saloon returns came down to 4s. and second class to 3s. The price was even said to include a free bottle of beer. The Steam Packet Company, with its fleet of eleven vessels and its long experience of this specialised trade, was much better equipped to stand the strain. The *Queen Victoria*, the *Prince of Wales* and the *Empress Queen* led the attack. Racing, with level starts from either station, was once more resumed, and there was much local enthusiasm as crowds watched for the winning arrivals. The Steam Packet Company had much the better of the contests and the major share of the traffic.

It was an unequal and expensive struggle; Higginbottom's company made heavy losses. The century turned; the annual traffic was vast compared with the early days; it had risen to 400,000 with Manx businessmen predicting confidently — and correctly — that the million would soon be reached. And of that 400,000 the Isle of Man Steam Packet Company took by far the largest number.

His several other enterprises may have flourished, but Higginbottom was losing steadily as a shipper in the Manx trade. He died in December, 1902, leaving one particular loss in liquidation behind him.

So in 1903 the pattern was repeated. Of the assets that were sold from the failure the *Calais/Douvres* was collected by the Steam Packet Company. It joined the fleet as the *Mona* (III) and served until 1909. It was the last paddle-steamer bought by the company.

After the collapse of Higginbottom's venture the Steam Packet Company once more had little competition on its main passenger route. Small cargo ships operated and still operate

A busy scene at Victoria Pier in the early days of this century. The steamers are Midland Railway's *Londonderry* (left) on the Heysham service and the Steam Packet's *Tynwald* (III) on the main route to Liverpool.

from Castletown and Ramsey but they are hardly in direct rivalry with the larger company. For some years, too, there were other services; the London Midland and Scottish Railway had a route between Heysham and Douglas, and there was a service between Llandudno and Douglas, operated by the Liverpool and North Wales Steamship Company. Again, these only carried a small proportion of the Manx trade.

At the outbreak of World War I the Steam Packet Company had a fleet of 15 vessels; it needed them, for in 1913 it had carried more than 1,100,000 passengers, such was the boom in Manx tourism. The adventurous and over-eager businessmen who had gambled in the Manx share and property syndicates of the late 1890's proved themselves to have been justified in what had seemed at the time to be excessive optimism.

The war took a heavy toll. Eleven of the fleet's steamers had been drafted into active service. By the time those that survived had been returned the fleet had a passenger carrying capacity of less than 8,000 against a prewar total of nearly 20,000. Details of the Company's record in World War I are given in Chapter Four.

There was at once an urgent need for more ships. The Admiralty had originally purchased the *Viking* and not merely commandeered it from the Company; now it was bought back. In the reshuffle of shipping that went on when peace came, the Steam Packet Company was able to buy five more ships in the second-hand market, bringing its fleet up to something approaching strength. It was a change in policy, for apart from the occasional charter and the three vessels collected from defeated rivals, the company had always commissioned its own ships from the builders; this ensured it the right craft for the shallow Manx harbours.

In 1928, ten years after the end of the War, the L.M.S. gave up the Douglas - Heysham route and the Steam Packet Company took over this service. More passenger accommodation was needed so the *Duke of Cornwall* and the *Antrim* were purchased from the railway company and added to the Manx fleet. In the same year the directors bought in the *Victoria* that had been built for the cross-Channel traffic of the South Eastern and Chatham Railway.

The L.M.S. and its predecessors had operated its Heysham to Douglas route for 24 years, since 1904. With the decision to relinquish the service the Steam Packet Company was again left in sole charge of the Manx passenger trade for almost another fifty years. Two private companies have run a small cargo and container service into the island and specialised coasters and tankers have made regular scheduled calls at Douglas with oil products, liquid gas, grain, and various bulk cargoes. But by far the major tonnage in the Manx trade, its car ferrying and for many more years the whole of its passenger trade, were borne by the Steam Packet Company.

In 1969 and 1970 a company named Norwest Hovercraft operated a service between Fleetwood and Douglas. For its first season it chartered the *Stella Marina*, from the Baltic which proved to be a very popular and succesful ship. The following year the Company was unable to charter the same vessel and instead bought the *Lochiel* (IV) from David MacBrayne Ltd., for whom she had been operating mainly to Islay from West Loch Tarbert. She was renamed *Norwest Laird* but her season was far from a success. There were difficulties in maintaining the sailing schedule owing to mechanical failures and the Company finally went into liquidation.

Stella Marina

Norwest Laird.

Since then one more concern has started up in the Island trade. Manx Line, a locally registered company, planned a roll-on roll-off car ferry service between Douglas and Heysham to operate from early in the 1978 tourist season. A Spanish ship, the *Monte Castillo*, was acquired and major adaptations were put in hand. Manx Line was responsible for the substantial cost of the link-span landing stage at Douglas, in addition to its involvement in the purchase and alterations to the ship. However, industrial and other troubles soon beset the *Manx Viking*, (as she was renamed) while she was being modified in a yard in Scotland, and eventually, instead of opening the service in early June, 1978, she appeared at the end of August. The passenger service was operated for only two weeks and then had to be withdrawn. After some repairs to the vessel a cargo-only service was operated. It was obvious that the new line had difficulties, but it was taken over by James Fisher & Company, the well-known Lancashire firm of ship brokers and specialised ship owners, with long experience of the British coastal trade. It was soon learned that behind Fisher's was Sealink (U.K.) Limited, which operates a large fleet of cross-Channel ferries and is answerable to the British Railways Board. Sealink acquired 60 per cent of Manx Line equity, leaving Fisher's with the balance.

Then came the next crisis. In a south-easterly gale the link-span was torn from its anchorage in December, 1978, severely damaging the pier and the unit itself. Once more the service was interrupted. The *Manx Viking* was sent to Belfast for structural alterations and overhaul and two small cargo vessels were used to maintain a container service between Douglas and Heysham. The link-span unit was salvaged and eventually towed back to its builders at New Ross in Ireland for repair. The *Manx Viking* returned to service in May, 1979, but in place of the landing stage a temporary platform and bridge alongside the Edward Pier enabled her to carry vehicles, but not heavy lorries. The link-span unit was towed back from Ireland, reinstated in June 1979 and *Manx Viking* resumed her service for all types of vehicles.

CHAPTER THREE: *The Fleet*

IN CONSULTATION WITH THE SUPERINTENDENT Engineer of the Company the technical figures given in this chapter have been arrived at after a study of the Steam Packet Company's own fleet list, transcripts taken from the original entries in the Register General of Shipping and Seamen, and importantly, from the marine engineering records in the Douglas offices. The lengths of the individual ships are given between the perpendiculars, as defined in Lloyd's Register of Shipping, the tonnages given are gross, while the horsepower, first nominal and then indicated or brake, has been checked back with the engineering records. Where there are discrepancies the figures finally given here are based on the performance reports of each ship.

1. *Mona's Isle* (I). No official number. Wooden paddle-steamer. Built 1830 by John Wood & Co., Glasgow, and launched on June 30. Cost £7,052. Gross tonnage 200; length 116′; beam 19′; depth 10′. The engine and boiler were by Robert Napier of Glasgow, and attracted considerable attention as Napier's work was considered very advanced for its day. The boiler

Mona's Isle (I)

produced a pressure of 15 pounds per square inch, and the engine was one of the earliest examples of the side-lever type. It was really the familiar beam engine of that era adapted for marine use. It was of 100 nominal horsepower and produced a speed of 8½ knots. The side-lever became the most popular type of engine for marine purposes and was adopted for use in ocean going vessels until 1850. Considered both fast and handsome, *Mona's Isle* was schooner rigged with a standing bowsprit; she was square sterned, carvel built, and carried false galleries and female bust figure. She had a tall funnel amidships, and the Manx symbol was on her paddle boxes. A design feature was the long bowsprit and clipper bow. Under the command of William Gill she established the Manx company's superiority over the rival St. George's Company. She was sold for breaking up for £580, having been bought by Robert Napier, who scrapped her in 1851. Previous efforts to sell the vessel had failed and Napier reboiled her in 1846 for £500.

Mona (I)   MANX MUSEUM

2.   *Mona* (I). No official number. Wooden paddle-steamer. Built 1831 by Robert Napier, Glasgow; came into service 1832. Tonnage 150; length 98′; beam 17′; depth 9′ 6″; speed 9 knots; nominal h.p. 70. Engine and boiler by Napier. Hurriedly ordered for the winter service in place of the larger *Mona's Isle*, which was soon considered too valuable to risk in storm conditions. Originally started on the Manx trade with Whitehaven; commenced winter service to Liverpool in October, 1832. Faster than the *Mona's Isle*, she could cut the Douglas to Liverpool run to 7½ hours. The smallest vessel in the Company's Fleet List. After rather less than 10 years service she was sold to a Liverpool company and then re-sold to the City of Dublin Company who converted her to a tug.

3.   *Queen of the Isle.*   No official number. Wooden paddle-steamer. Built by Robert Napier, Glasgow, in 1834, launched May 3, went into service from Douglas in September 1834. Gross tonnage 350; length 128′; beam 21′ 6″; depth 12′ 7″; speed 9½ knots; nominal h.p. 140. Schooner rigged with standing bowsprit, carvel built; stern design similar to the Steam Packet's two previous vessels. Said to be the fastest vessel on the Irish Sea in her day. On March 25, 1835, she collided with the steamer *Irishman* in the Mersey. Sold in 1845 after which she was converted into a sailing ship and was eventually lost off the Falkland Islands.

Queen of the Isle   MANX MUSEUM

King Orry (I)   MANX MUSEUM

4. *King Orry* (I). No. 21923. Wooden paddle-steamer. Built by J. Winram and Robert Napier and launched February 10, 1842. Cost £10,763. Tonnage 433; length 140′; beam 23′ 3″; depth 14′ 3″; speed 9½ knots; nominal h.p. 180. The last wooden vessel in the Steam Packet fleet and the only ship in its history to have been built in Douglas. Two masts, schooner rigged; standing bowsprit, square sterned, carvel built with sham galleries and male figurehead. Although the John Winram yard gets the credit it is probable that the building was supervised by Aitken of Liverpool, and the Douglas yard merely carried out the construction. Later in

1842 she was towed by *Mona's Isle* to Glasgow for engines to be fitted by Robert Napier. On joining the fleet her fastest run between Douglas and Liverpool was 6 hrs. 20 mins. and her average about 7 hrs. She was reboilered in 1847 for £3,000. In 1858 she was taken over by Napier in part payment for the *Douglas*; £5,000 was allowed as her value. She was then sold to the Greeks by Napier and traded in the eastern Mediterranean.

Ben-my-Chree (I)

5.   *Ben-my-Chree* (I).   No. 21922. Iron paddle-steamer. Built by Robert Napier at Glasgow in 1845. Cost £11,500. Tonnage 458; length 151′ 9″ between perpendiculars; beam 23′; depth 12′ 5″. Robert Napier's engine was taken from the *Queen of the Isle* before the vessel was sold and converted to a full rig sailing ship. The speed of the *Ben-my-Chree* is not recorded, but Napier's engine had produced a speed of 9½ knots in the earlier ship. It should be recorded that while the first registration of the *Ben-my-Chree* gives her tonnage as 458, the Company's Fleet List and other sources give it as 399. Boiler pressure had increased slightly in the 13 years since the start of the Steam Packet Company, and this vessel's was 20 p.s.i. After 15 years service she was disposed of in 1860, sent to Leith and sold by Tod and McGregor for £1,200. After many years service she was reported to be lying a hulk on the Bonny River, West Africa, 70 years after her launching.

6.   *Tynwald* (I).   No. 21921. Iron paddle-steamer. Built Glasgow 1846 by R. Napier & Son. Cost £21,500. 700 tons; length 188′; beam 27′; depth 13′ 6″. There is no record of the speed of this vessel or its nominal horsepower. She has the dubious distinction of being the first Steam Packet vessel whose launch was delayed for some time by a strike in the shipbuilding yard — as reported by the directors in 1846. The first, but by no means the last. Three masts, with the funnel abaft the paddle boxes. Conspicuous feature; a full length figurehead of a Manx Scandinavian king in armour. She was a reliable ship. A local newspaper described her as being "as sure as a mountain goat". During the winter season in 1850 she was chartered to

Tynwald (I)   MANX MUSEUM

The arrival at Douglas of the new Lieut-Governor, Francis Piggott and his family on *Tynwald* (I)
(Capt. Alexander McQueen) on 14th February, 1861.   BASNETT COLLECTION

go to the Mediterranean and called at Gibraltar, Genoa and Leghorn, making the round trip in 30 days. In December 1863 she was in collision with the Naval brig *Wild Wave*, the settlement after a long wrangle costing the Steam Packet Company £1,128. Back in December 1846, when on charter to the Liverpool and Belfast Company she collided with the mail steamer *Urgent* and damaged a paddle box. Captain Gill was exonerated by the directors: the accident occurred during dense fog. £386 was later noted in the minutes as the cost of repairs to the vessel. This did not prevent the directors from later claiming £2,004 in compensation for damage and loss of earnings, and then, on legal advice, settling for £1,489. In 1886 she was sold for £5,000 to Caird & Co. in part payment for *Tynwald* (II).

Mona's Queen (I)   MANX MUSEUM

7.   *Mona's Queen* (I).   No. 21930. Iron paddle-steamer. Built and engined by J. and G. Thompson of Clydebank, and launched from Glasgow in 1853. 600 tons; length 186'; beam 27'; depth 13'; speed and horsepower not recorded. Carried a figurehead of Queen Victoria. The first steamer to break away from the Company's long association with Napier. This vessel's cost is not recorded but a reference in the company's old minute books suggests it was under £14,000. In 1855 she was lengthened (details not recorded) at a cost of £2,111. The vessel appeared to have an uneventful career except for a collision with the steamer *Sligo* in January 1862 in the River Mersey. The official inquiry went against the Steam Packet Company who had to pay approximately £300 in damages and costs. The Captain was accordingly reduced from Second Class Master to Third and his pay cut from £275 to £250. After ten years' service the directors decided to sell the ship and offered it to Cunard, Wilson and Co. for £20,000. The offer was declined. Negotiations started with a Whitehaven company for a sale at £14,000. Midway through 1864 the Manx directors admitted that they could not sell the vessel. She continued in the trade until broken up in 1880.

8.   *Douglas* (I).   No. 20683. Iron paddle-steamer. Built by Robert Napier & Co. in Glasgow in 1858. Engines and boiler work also by Napier. Cost £17,500, plus an allowance of £5,000 from Napier's for the *King Orry*. Tonnage 700; length 205'; beam 26'; depth 14'; speed 17 knots; nominal horse power believed to be 260.
     The first IOMSP steamer with a straight stem, no fiddle bow and no figurehead, longer

Douglas (I) from a drawing by John Nicholson.

and faster than her forerunners and built to help meet the steady increase in passenger traffic. Said to have done 17¼ knots on her trial trip and then to have crossed from Liverpool to Douglas in 4 hrs. 20 mins. Claimed to be the fastest steamer then afloat. She attracted wide attention and her speed made her a strong candidate for more advanced adventures. While in the Steam Packet Company's colours the only event of interest, apart from the way she broke the record for the home run, was her collision with the brig *Dido*, which cost the company approximately £400 in damages. At one time she was chartered to Hendersons of Belfast for three weeks for the then notable fee of £200 a week. After only four years service she was sold nominally to Cunard, Wilson and Co., but really to the Confederate Agents, Fraser Trenholm and Co. for £24,000. Painted grey and renamed the *Margaret and Jessie*, she was an ideal blockade runner in the American Civil War. She was then owned by the Charleston Import and Export Co. but was gunned down and driven ashore near Nassau on June 1, 1863, by a Union gunboat. A few days later she escaped although damaged, went back to blockade running and was later captured. Some records maintained that after she had been driven ashore and had escaped to Nassau, she took no further part in the American Civil War and her engines were said to be seen rusting on the Nassau beach as late as July, 1926. The official history of the ship in the library of the Department of the Navy, Washington, D.C., clarifies the conflicting reports. The vessel did go back to work and was captured as a blockade runner on November 5, 1863, bought by the Navy from the New York Prize Court, and commissioned as the *Gettysburg* on May 2, 1864, at the New York Navy Yard. She had been armed with a 30-pounder Parrott gun, two 12-pounders, and four 24-pounder howitzers. Her tonnage was given as 950 and she was apparently lengthened by 16 feet to 221 feet. When commissioned she had a ship's complement of 96. She joined the North Atlantic Blockading Squadron and captured several ships that were attempting to run supplies to the South.

On December 24, 1864, the *Gettysburg* took part in the notable sea-to-shore attack on Fort Fisher, assisting in the heavy naval bombardment, coming close in to cover troops landing for the actual assault, and using her boats to carry troops to the beaches. She was in action again three weeks later when the assault was repeated and was successful, this time in association with land forces. For the remainder of the Civil War the paddle-steamer went back to her blockade duties. She was on active service in 1868, protecting American interests in the Caribbean, helping to lay submarine cables and doing survey work. In 1875 she did important work for the Hydrographic Office, compiling navigation charts of the seas in the West Indies. In November, 1876, she set off for Europe and spent two years doing surveys in the Mediterranean, taking observations along the entire coastline of Italy, as well as the south of France, the Adriatic islands, and the coasts of Turkey, Eygpt, and North Africa. In the course of this duty the U.S. Navy record states that she visited nearly every port in the Mediterranean. On April 22, 1879, she rescued the crew of a small vessel that had hit the rocks outside Genoa. She then went into harbour. Her plates were corroded from 21 years of almost uninterrupted service and her machinery was weakened. She was decommissioned on May 6, 1879, and sold two days later. The *Gettysburg*'s active record was an outstanding testimonial to the craftsmanship of the Robert Napier Company back in Scotland.

Mona's Isle (II)   *Ellan Vannin*

9.   *Mona's Isle* (II).   No. 27260. Iron paddle-steamer. Built by Tod and McGregor, Glasgow, and joined the fleet in June 1860. Cost £10,673. Name changed to *Ellan Vannin* on November 16, 1883, after she had been converted to a twin-screw steamer. 339 tons; length 198' 6"; beam 22' 2"; depth 10' 7". She was considered one of the most profitable of the early vessels owned by the Company. As *Ellan Vannin* she could carry 106 first class passengers on deck and 28 in cabins, and 140 third class with 25 in cabins, a total of 299. She had a crew of 14. When launched the *Mona's Isle* (II) had a speed of 12 knots and an i.h.p. of 600. She was important in the history of the Company as the first of their vessels to be fitted with oscillating engines. These were made by Tod and McGregor. Until 1860 the Company had always used the side -lever engine so favoured by Napier. The oscillating engine possessed a number of advantages over the side-lever: it occupied less space and had fewer working parts; there was no connecting rod; the upper end of the piston rod was fitted with a bearing which worked directly on to the crankpin. The cylinder was placed vertically under the crankshaft and could pivot through a small arc, permitting the rod to follow the movements of the crank. She

served as the *Mona's Isle* for 23 years. In 1883 she was converted to a twin-screw vessel driven by a two-cylinder compound engine made by Westray, Copeland and Co. at Barrow. Her boiler pressure was raised to 80 pounds p.s.i. She gave 26 more years fleet service and became the main mail carrier from Ramsey sailing to Whitehaven, Liverpool and Scotland. In December 1891 she completed a special overhaul at the Naval Construction Works at Barrow, costing £2,913. She was considered an exceptionally fine vessel in bad weather, carrying out the daily mail contract when other vessels were safe in harbour. On December 3, 1909, she left Ramsey for Liverpool with 15 passengers, a crew of 21, mail and cargo. A severe north-westerly gale reaching Force 12 blew up as she was approaching the Mersey. She passed the Bar before seven in the morning but foundered in what was officially described as one of the worst storms ever experienced. She is believed to have been swept by heavy seas and filled, sinking by the stern, the action of the waves breaking her bows. All aboard were lost. News of the disaster reached Douglas on the Friday evening and the directors sat in almost continuous session until the Monday. Communication was by telegram and information was tardy. Then the Liverpool agent reported that two lifebuoys, bags of turnips and a piano had been seen floating near the Formby lightship. That was the first real news. It was five days after the ship went down that the first bodies were recovered. The official inquiry referred to waves 24 feet high and declared the ship to have been in good condition and fully seaworthy; there was no criticism of Company, Master or crew. The name *Ellan Vannin* was never repeated in the Company's Fleet List. A fund was set up for the dependents of those lost in the tragedy, with £1,000 immediately donated by the Steam Packet Company. The crew of 21 included one woman, a Mrs. Callister, of Crosby, Isle of Man, who left one child. The 20 men were survived by 18 widows and 70 children. All but two of the crew lived on the Isle of Man. Five of the passengers came from the mainland, the rest from the north of the island. The last beneficiary from the fund was a Miss Benson of Ramsey, the daughter of one of the crew. She was 20 when the disaster occurred and was in very poor health. It was most unlikely that she would be the last to benefit from the fund, but she was, dying in 1974 at the age of 85.

10. *Snaefell* (I).   No. 45468. Iron paddle-steamer. Built and engined by Caird & Co., Greenock, and launched 1863. Cost £22,000. Tonnage 700; length 236'; beam 26'; depth 14'. She was the first of three very similar paddle steamers built for the Steam Packet Company by Caird & Co., and further discarding the original Napier side-lever engine design. All three

Snaefell (I)

ships — *Snaefell* (I), *Douglas* (II) and *Tynwald* (II) — were driven by two-cylinder oscillating engines with a nominal horsepower of 240 in the case of the first of them, *Snaefell* (I). Fast for her day, she could do the Douglas-Liverpool run in ten minutes under 4½ hours. She was reboilered in 1869 for £3,500. She was grounded in 1871, following which the Captain offered to resign. The shareholders asked the board to reappoint him. After much discussion Thomas Corlett was not reappointed, and the command was given to Thomas Lewis — at a salary of £225 a year, reduced to half pay during lay up. After only 12 years with the Manx fleet she was sold to the Royal Netherlands Steamship Company of Amsterdam for £15,500 in 1875. She was renamed the *Stad Breda* and plied between Sheerness and Flushing. In 1888 she was sold for scrapping.

Douglas (II)   MANX MUSEUM

11. *Douglas* (II).   No. 45470. Iron paddle-steamer. Built by Caird & Co. of Greenock and launched 1864. Engines by Caird. Cost £24,869. Tonnage 709; length 227'; beam 26'; depth 14'; speed not recorded; indicated horsepower 1400. Boiler pressure 25 pounds p.s.i. Sister ship to the *Snaefell* (I) and *Tynwald* (II). She had one funnel forward and one aft of the paddle-boxes with the main mast close to the after funnel. She was reboilered in 1869 for £4,000. A successful ship in the company's Fleet with an uneventful career. Disposed of by auction in 1888, together with *Tynwald* (II) — see Fleet List No. 12. The two ships together realised £26,644.

12. *Tynwald* (II).   No. 45474. Iron paddle-steamer. Built and engined by Caird & Co. of Greenock, and launched 1866. Cost £26,000. Tonnage 696; length 240'; beam 26'; depth 14'; no speed recorded; nominal h.p. 280. Both funnels aft of the paddleboxes; the main mast close to the after funnel. A fast ship, in 1882 she had a thorough overhaul being fitted with new boilers, surface condenser and new decks, which with repairs to engines, cost £11,219. She was disposed of in 1888.

Tynwald (II) arriving at Llandudno, 19th July, 1887.   REV. R. O. YEARSLEY

13. *King Orry* (II). No. 45479. Iron paddle-steamer. Built by R. Duncan & Co., Port Glasgow, 1871, with engines by Rankin and Blackmore. Boiler work by R. Duncan. Cost £26,000. Crew of 47; accommodation for 1104 passengers. Original tonnage 809, later increased to 1,104. Length 260′; beam 29′ 4″; depth 14′ 7″. Her original speed was 15 knots. She was refitted by Fairfield & Co. in 1888, at a cost of £8,246, and lengthened by 30 feet. At the same time she was reboiled by J. Jones & Co. for £4,080, giving her a new boiler pressure of 110 pounds p.s.i. This thorough refit increased her speed from 15 to 17 knots and her indicated horsepower to 4,000. In 1895 she was given a complete electric lighting installation costing £575. Her diagonal compound engines now had a stroke of 78 inches with a high pressure cylinder of 52 inches and low pressure 92. She was a handsome vessel; and after 41 years service she was broken up in Llanerchymor in 1912. At that time she had the longest service record in the Steam Packet fleet history.

King Orry (II)   MANX MUSEUM

Ben-my-Chree (II)   MANX MUSEUM

14.   *Ben-my-Chree* (II).   No. 67288. Iron paddle-steamer. Built in 1875 by the Barrow Shipbuilding Company, Barrow-in-Furness. Engines and boilers by the shipbuilders. Cost £38,000. Original tonnage 1030, but increased to 1192 after refit. Length 310′; beam 31′; depth 13′; speed 14 knots; indicated horsepower 2300. She was fitted with two oscillating two-cylinder engines of 65 inches diameter, with a 90 inch stroke. The largest ship built for the Company to date, but slow, being 2 knots below her originally agreed speed, despite modifications to the boilers. Reboilered in 1884 she was altered to carry four funnels, in pairs fore and aft of the paddle-boxes. This made her the only four-funnelled vessel in the history of the line. After an uneventful career of 31 years she was scrapped by T. W. Ward and Company at Morecambe.

Snaefell (II)   MANX MUSEUM

15. *Snaefell* (II). No. 67289. Iron paddle-steamer. Built 1876 by Caird & Co., Glasgow, with engines and boilers by Caird. Cost £28,250. New boilers by Fawcett, Preston and Company of Liverpool, fitted by Jones and Sons of Liverpool in 1885 for £8,512. Tonnage 849; length 251' 3"; beam 29' 3"; depth 14' 1"; speed 15 knots; indicated h.p. 1700. A smaller vessel than her immediate predecessors but equally successful. Steaming to Ardrossan from Douglas in August, 1892, in hazy weather, she collided with the Norwegian vessel *Kaleb*. Both ships were damaged but the *Snaefell* (II) went to the Fairfield yards under own steam. The subsequent repairs cost £1,298. Legislation followed and finally the Edinburgh court decided that both ships were to blame. In 1895 she was fitted out with electric lighting for £425. The Zeeland Steamship Company of Holland who had bought *Snaefell* (I) and had successfully used her for 13 years, sometimes chartered *Snaefell* (II). After 38 years steady service the paddler was disposed of in 1904.

16. *Mona* (II). No. 76302. Iron single-screw steamer. Built in 1878 by William Laird & Co., Birkenhead, with engine and boilers by Laird. Cost £19,500. Tonnage 526, later altered to 562. Length 200'; beam 26'; depth 13'. An important vessel in the Steam Packet Company's history for she was not only the first single-screw ship of the line but she was fitted with vertical compound engines and proved much more economical to run and better suited to winter service than the paddle steamers that had previously made up the Company's fleet. She had a nominal h.p. of 160 and a speed of 13 knots. She was both a passenger and cargo vessel designed especially for the winter service. When only five years old she was at anchor in fog in the Formby Channel at the approaches to Liverpool when she was run into by the *Rita*, a Spanish steamer, and she sank almost at once. The crew together with two women, who were the only passengers, took to the lifeboats and were saved. Some were picked up by the Formby Lightship. The *Rita*, which had been damaged, was outward bound from Liverpool but returned to port. Ironically in 1881 Hughes & Co., brokers of Liverpool, who had foreign customers for reasonably new screw steamers, had offered £18,000 for the vessel, but the IOMSP refused — their price being £21,000.

Mona (II)

Fenella (I)   MANX MUSEUM

17.   *Fenella* (I). No.76303. Iron twin-screw steamer. Built in 1881 by the Barrow Shipbuilding Company of Barrow-in-Furness, who also built the engines and boilers. Tonnage 564; length 200′; beam 26′; depth 13′; Cost £18,750. Certified accommodation for crew of 28, with 504 passengers. She served in the Steam Packet fleet for 48 years, including service in World War I. At least one mercantile marine authority considers that from a steamship development viewpoint the *Fenella* (I) was the most interesting vessel built for the Company since the first vessel in 1830. She had an indicated horsepower of 1,200 and a speed of 14 knots, with a boiler pressure of 85 pounds p.s.i. She was possibly the first, but if not, at least one of the very earliest twin-screw steamers. She was driven by two sets of vertical compound engines each with cylinder bores of 23 and 42 inches, with a stroke of 24 inches. Her work demonstrated that high steam pressure with compound engines, having a higher piston speed than would have been practicable in a paddle steamer, gave her greater economy in performance. She was overhauled in 1894 and a full electric light system fitted — 56 lights in all. The *Peveril* (Fleet List No. 19) was fitted with electricity at the same time, the electrical contractors being J. W. Holmes of Liverpool. The bill for the two installations was £505. Primarily a cargo ship, intended to do passenger runs as relief service in winter, it could possibly be claimed that she was worked harder than any other of the company's ships in her day. She served on every route the Steam Packet Company then operated, including the Peel-Belfast run which is one of a number no longer operated. For her war service see Chapter Four. On one occasion she made six round trips between Douglas and Liverpool and then took troops to Kingstown, all in three days. She was the first Manx ship to lose a life from the deck, when on January 4th, 1899 three passengers were carried overboard by a wave after refusing to go below. She was sold for £2,290 in 1929, after 48 successful years with the Company.

18.   *Mona's Isle* (III).   No. 76304. Steel paddle-steamer, built by Caird & Co. at Greenock in 1882, with engines and boilers by the same company. Cost £58,700. Gross tonnage 1564; length 330′ 7″; beam 38′ 1″; depth 15′ 1″. She was allowed 1561 passengers and 56 crew. The engines of this ship produced an i.h.p. of 4,500 and a speed of 18 knots. They were quite remarkable for

their day. The oscillating engine had slowly developed from low pressure jet condensing with all the demerits that a salt water intake involved, to higher pressure surface condensing that was the forerunner of the turbine circulating system of today. These were the first high pressure engines of this type to be adopted by the Steam Packet Company. They worked at a boiler pressure of 90 lbs. p.s.i. The stroke was 90 inches, with the high pressure cylinder 65 inches in diameter and the low pressure 112 inches. The l.p. cylinder was said to be heavier and larger than any other fitted to a paddle-steamer. *Mona's Isle* (III) was the largest, best appointed, and most expensive steamer in the Company's history up to that time. Exceptionally fast in her day she could reach Liverpool from Douglas in 3hr. 35 min. She was the first of five rather similar steel paddle-steamers added to the fleet between 1882 and 1889. In 1895 she was fitted with electric light for £600. She had been structuraly damaged in heavy seas in 1885; in September 1892 she went aground on Scarlett Point, Castletown, while rounding the south of the Island, homeward bound from Dublin, and she was fast aground for two days. In 1915 she was sold to the Admiralty and saw much active service in World War I. (See Chapter Five.) The Company did not buy her back after the war.

Mona's Isle (III)

19.   *Peveril* (I).   No. 76307. Steel; twin-screw. Built 1884 by the Barrow Shipbuilding Company of Barrow-in-Furness, with engines and boilers by the same company. Cost £20,000. Tonnage 561/595; length 207'; beam 26'; depth 13'; speed 13½ knots; indicated h.p. 1200. When ten years old she was fitted with electric lights; 57 points were installed. In 1895 these installations were considered so successful that it was decided to instal a similar lighting system to the *Mona's Isle* (III), the *King Orry* (II), and the *Snaefell* (II). Accommodation for 30 crew, a sister ship of the *Fenella* (I) intended for general cargo work in the main season and for

Peveril (I) leaving Ramsey.

Mona's Queen (II) arriving at Llandudno in 1923

F. C. THORNLEY

passenger service relief in winter. After 15 years in the fleet she was sunk off Douglas on September 16, 1899. Although it was a night with excellent visibility the *Monarch*, sailing from Workington to Cardiff, and the *Peveril* were crossing on a collision course. Neither ship appeared to alter course and the *Monarch* rammed the *Peveril* amidships, flooding the engine room. The *Peveril* sank in 40 minutes, but there were no casualties, the entire crew and the one solitary passenger being taken aboard the *Monarch*, which landed them at Douglas.

20. *Mona's Queen* (II). No. 76308. Steel paddle-steamer. Built in 1885 by the Barrow Shipbuilding Company of Barrow-in-Furness, with engines and boilers by the same company. Cost £55,000. Tonnage 1559; length 320′ 1″; beam 38′ 3″; depth 14′ 5″; speed 19 knots. Her engine design attracted attention when she was first built, for she had a set of compound surface condensing cylinder engines giving 5,000 i.h.p. Her boiler steam pressure was 87 pounds p.s.i. She was the last ship built for the Company to be fitted with oscillating engines. Certified for crew of 51 and 1465 passengers. The second of the large paddle-steamers that dominated the Steam Packet Company's fleet until the Company turned solely to screw driven vessels from 1905. She started on the Fleetwood-Douglas service but was transferred to the main home run to help meet and beat the competition of the Isle of Man, Liverpool and Manchester Company. She was fast and in her first season often steamed from Douglas to the Wyre Light at Fleetwood in under three hours. Most sources give her speed as 18 knots, but her record with the Registrar General of Shipping and Seamen says 19. In 1888 she was overhauled at Barrow and fitted with new paddles and superheated. She had a most distinguished record in World War I (See Chapter 5). On returning to the Steam Packet Company she continued on normal duties and was the last paddle-steamer in the Company's fleet when she was sold in 1929 for £5,920 to Smith & Co. of Port Glasgow.

21. *Prince of Wales*. No. 93381. Steel paddle-steamer. Built in 1887 by Fairfield & Co., Govan; engines and boilers by the same company. Purchased on November 23, 1888 by the Steam Packet Company from the Isle of Man, Liverpool and Manchester Steamship Company. Cost £155,000, including cost of the *Queen Victoria* (Fleet List No. 22). Tonnage 1568; length 330′; beam 39′ 1″; depth 15′ 2″; speed (in trials on measured mile) 24.25 knots. Accommodation for 1546 passengers and 69 crew. The *Prince of Wales* and her sister ship *Queen Victoria* had boiler steam pressure of 110 pounds p.s.i. They had compound engines of 6,500 i.h.p. at 40.5 r.p.m. in service of the type known as the coupled two crankshaft engine. The crankshaft was connected at the cranks by a drag link, the object of which was to get the two

Prince of Wales   MANX MUSEUM

cranks at right angles, one engine driving the valve gear of the other. The h.p. cylinder was horizontal and the l.p. diagonal to the centre of the shaft. The two cylinders were 61 and 112 inches in diameter with 78" stroke. So successful were these two ships that a number of other companies adopted the engine design for cross-channel work. This very fast ship had beaten the best vessels in the Steam Packet fleet in the short rivalry on the Douglas route, and she was a most valuable addition to the fleet of the surviving line. She once steamed from the Rock Light to Douglas Head in 2 hrs. 59 min., an average speed of 23¼ knots. In August, 1894, she collided with and sank the steamer *Hibernia*, two of whose crew were lost; the third man was picked up by the Steam Packet ship. Some months later the Manx vessel was held to blame and a claim of £1,750 had to be accepted. She was sold to the Admiralty in 1915 and during her service in World War I (See Chapter 5) her name was changed to *Prince Edward*. After the war she was sold to T. C. Pas for £5,600 and broken up at Scheveningen, Holland.

22.   *Queen Victoria*.   No. 93379. Steel paddle-steamer. Built, with engines and boilers, at Govan, by Fairfield & Co. in 1887, and bought in 1888 from the Isle of Man, Liverpool and Manchester line at the same time as her sister ship the *Prince of Wales*. Gross Tonnage 1568; length 330'; beam 39' 1"; depth 15' 2"; speed 21 knots; 6500 i.h.p. Crew of 69 and accommodation for 1546 passengers. On her delivery run from Glasgow on May 21, 1887 she averaged 22½ knots in heavy seas; said to be the then record run between the Clyde and Liverpool. Not as fast as her sister ship she became a very valuable member of the Steam Packet fleet, and was finally requisitioned by the Admiralty and sold to them on January 28, 1915. (See Chapter 5). At the end of the war she was sold to Ambacht in Holland in April 1920 for £5,450.

Queen Victoria   MANX MUSEUM

Tynwald (III)

23. *Tynwald* (III). No. 95755. Steel ship with twin-screws, built by Fairfield at Govan, 1891. Cost £58,683. Gross tonnage 937; length 265′ between perpendiculars; beam 34′; depth 14′; speed 18 knots. With this vessel the Company made another move forward in its marine engineering design — the triple-expansion engine. Her two boilers had steam pressure of 160 pounds p.s.i., and each boiler was fired by eight furnaces. She had bunker room for 120 tons of coal. The two sets of triple-expansion engines developed 3,800 i.h.p., at 120 r.p.m. For the first time in the history of the Steam Packet Company the builder's specification included a full installation of electric lighting. She had a certificate for 679 first class passengers and 225 third, a total of 904 in all, and a crew of 50. Fast for her size she could hold her own with the *Queen Victoria*. She worked the seasonal Douglas-Ardrossan run. On April 6, 1893, while at anchor in the Mersey, she was run into by the steamer *Lotus* and extensively damaged. In 1912 she opened a service from Douglas to Whitehaven calling at Ramsey, and was also used as a winter vessel on the main home run. Her World War I service was unusual (See Chapter 5), and she later returned to the Steam Packet Company who used her in excursion runs to Blackpool. It was intended to scrap her in 1933 and she was laid up. In December 1934 she was sold to R. A. Colby Cubbin of the Isle of Man, who renamed her *Western Isles* and planned to convert her into a private yacht. She was for some years lying in Glasgow and was requisitioned by the Admiralty in 1940, renamed *Eastern Isles* and served as an auxiliary in World War II. She returned to her owner in 1947 and was broken up at Genoa in 1951. She had then been afloat for 60 years, and in the Steam Packet Company's service for 42 of them; a good record for any ship.

24. *Empress Queen*. No. 95759. Steel paddle-steamer. Built, with engines and boilers, by Fairfields at Govan in 1897. Cost £130,000. Tonnage 2140; length 360′ 1″; beam 42′ 3″; depth 17′; speed 21½ knots. The engine design was very advanced for its day. She was the largest and fastest paddle-driven cross-channel steamer ever to be built. She could take a crew of 95 and

Empress Queen

1994 passengers. She had a boiler steam pressure of 140 pounds p.s.i., and her two diagonal three-crank compound type engines developed 10,000 i.h.p. One h.p. cylinder was 68″ in diameter and was placed centrally with the two l.p. cylinders of 92″ diameter on either side. The stroke was 84″. Her usual running speed was 44 r.p.m. These engines and paddle wheels were claimed to be the heaviest ever placed in a paddle steamer, with one paddle shaft wheel alone weighing 70 tons. Sixteen firemen worked at her 32 furnaces. It was intended to call her the *Douglas* but the name *Empress Queen* was adopted in honour of Queen Victoria's Jubilee. The first IOMSP ship to be fitted with radio — August 19, 1903. This was the last paddle steamer ordered to be built for the line, and she was a record breaker for her day. On September 13, 1897, she went from the Rock Light to Douglas Head in 2 hr. 57 min., the fastest time then recorded. For her World War I service see Chapter 5. On February 1, 1916, she was stranded in fog off Bembridge, on the Isle of Wight, and she broke up. There were 1,300 troops aboard at the time but no lives were lost.

25.   *Douglas* (III).   No. 94515. Steel built; single-screw. Original name *Dora* and built in 1889 by Robert Napier & Co. of Glasgow for the London and South Western Railway Company. Bought by the Steam Packet on July 26, 1901 for £13,500. Napier's were also responsible for engines and boilers. Tonnage 774; length 240′; beam 30′; depth 15′ 2″; speed 15 knots; 2,000 i.h.p. Certified accommodation for 33 crew and 506 passengers. The *Douglas* (III) was a departure in Steam Packet practice. Until 1901 all its ships had been ordered and built for it, with the exception of the two eminently suitable *Prince of Wales* and *Queen Victoria*, which had been bought in after their owners had unsuccessfully tilted at the Manx trade. The *Douglas*, however, was a straight purchase to fill the gap left when the *Peveril* was sunk in 1899. The ship had been working the Southampton service to the Channel Islands and was thus very well suited to the Irish Sea trade. In November 1903 she collided with and sank the *City of Lisbon* in

the Mersey. She was also used for the winter services and she continued trading between the Island and the mainland during the First World War, playing a valuable part in maintaining the island's lifeline. Returning to her normal work she was sunk on August 16, 1923. She had pulled out of the Brunswick Dock in the River Mersey at the start of her voyage to Douglas, and was attempting to cross the bows of the *Artemisia*, a ship of 5,731 tons, inward bound from Java to Liverpool with a cargo of sugar. She struck the *Douglas* amidships but the Duty Officer of the *Artemisia*, a London ship owned by H. M. Thomson of Edinburgh, prevented loss of life by keeping his engines going and holding his bows into the Douglas's side, so keeping her afloat until all crew and 15 passengers were taken off safely. The Manx ship then sank and her wreck was destroyed nearly four months later. The collision was followed by a lengthy and expensive legal wrangle in which it was revealed that the *Artemisia* was waiting her turn to enter the dock and was lying a thousand feet off the entrance with just sufficient seaway to stem the flood tide. The *Douglas* left the dock, turned into the tidal water intending to go round the larger ship. The issue turned on seamanship and the Admiralty Court held that the *Douglas* was alone to blame. The case was heard on June 5, 1924.

The Steam Packet appealed against the decision and the appeal was allowed. This time the *Artemisia* was held to blame. Then came the final appeal to the House of Lords. The successful appeal was dismissed and their Lordships reversed the findings of the Appeal Court. The responsibility of the collision rested solely on the *Douglas*.

Douglas (III)   MANX MUSEUM

Mona (III)   MANX MUSEUM

26.   *Mona* (III).   No. 96575. Steel paddle-steamer, built by Fairfields of Govan in 1889 for the London, Chatham and Dover Railway Company and named *Calais/Douvres*, and sold by them to Higginbottom's Liverpool and Douglas Steamers, from whose liquidators the Steam Packet Company purchased her for £6,000 in July 1903, renaming her at the same time. Tonnage 1212; length 324′ 5″; beam 35′ 9″; depth 13′ 5″; speed 18 knots; indicated horsepower 5400. No speed is entered in her details in the Register of Shipping but her best run on trials averaged 18.86 knots. The IOMSP give it as 18 knots but she is said to have steamed from Dover to Calais in three minutes under the hour at an average of 22.6 knots. She could carry 1212 passengers and 59 crew. A double-ended vessel, she is mainly of interest as the last paddle-ship bought for the Steam Packet fleet. She was scrapped in 1909.

Viking   E. A. NURSE

27. *Viking.* No. 118604. Steel built; triple-screw turbine, built by Armstrong, Whitworth of Newcastle-on-Tyne in 1905, with turbines by Parsons. Cost £83,900. Tonnage 1957; length 350′; beam 42′; depth 17′ 3″; speed 22½ knots. Certified for crew of 80 and passenger accommodation for 1600. This was a notable Steam Packet ship, the first to be turbine-driven in the Company's history. Her three propellers were driven by three sets of Parsons direct-acting turbines, the higher pressure in the centre and the lower pressure in each wing. She had a boiler steam pressure of 160 pounds p.s.i., and her i.h.p. was 10,000. The astern turbines which operated on the wing propellers were incorporated in the low pressure casings. She remained in service until she became the last coal burning passenger ship in the Steam Packet Fleet. Although her registered speed was 22 knots, and the Company's own records claim 22½, she was in fact known to have made 24 on occasions. It was even said at one time that only the senior Cunard liners were faster and she was certainly the fastest vessel in the Manx trade. She recorded the then record time from Fleetwood to Douglas in 1907, doing the journey in 2 hours 22 minutes at an average speed of 23.2 knots. She was ordered and intended for the Fleetwood-Douglas service to oppose the old Midland Railway Company's *Manxman*, which was also a turbine steamer and which ran from Heysham to the Island. She did exceptional and important service in World War I, having been converted to a seaplane carrier (see Chapter 5). During this time her name was changed from *Viking* to *Vindex* (H.M.S.), reverting to *Viking* in July 1920. At the end of the war she was repurchased by the Steam Packet Company, refitted, and completed another ten years dominating the Fleetwood service until she moved to general duties in 1930. For the second time in her long life she was requisitioned in 1939 and had an adventurous time in World War II, including service during the landings in France on D-Day. (See Chapter 7.) Once more she returned to the Fleetwood service for the Steam Packet Company after a refit in June, 1945. Cammell Laird then over-hauled her at Birkenhead in 1949 and rebladed her turbines two years later. She finished her work on the Fleetwood service on August 14, 1954, and two days later went to Barrow under her own steam to be broken up by T. M. Ward after 49 years service. She had a long association with Fleetwood and to commemorate this her bell was formally presented to the Borough of Fleetwood.

28. *Ben-my-Chree* (III). No. 118605. Steel built; triple-screw turbine. Built in 1908 by Vickers Sons and Maxim, Barrow-in-Furness, who also built the turbines. Cost £112,100. Tonnage 2250; length 375′; beam 46′; depth 18′ 6″; speed 24½ knots. Passenger accommodation for 2,549; crew 119. The *Ben-my-Chree* (III) resulted from the great success of the *Viking*, built three years earlier. The Company quickly decided that a larger and more powerful turbine ship should be ordered for the Liverpool-Douglas service. She was driven by three turbines with a shaft h.p. of 14,000 and a boiler steam pressure of 170 pounds p.s.i. Her sustained speeds during her working life were expensive for those days. She used 95 tons of coal in one day's steaming. She was the fastest and most powerful ship ever built for the Steam Packet Company and an outstanding success during her short life; proudly described by the Manx Company at the time as "the fastest and most luxuriously appointed channel steamer afloat". Her normal service speed approached 24 knots but she achieved 24.5 on extended trails. In her first season between Liverpool and Douglas her average time between the Bar Lightship and the Head was 2 hr. 24 min. A year later she reduced this average by one minute. She was very much a record breaker, looking more like a miniature Cunarder than the conventional cross-channel ship. The *Ben-my-Chree*'s exceptional speed caused several stories to circulate about her. She was widely said to have achieved 26.9 knots, although her fastest run on trials over the measured mile was 24.5. It is most improbable that the vessel approached 27 knots except in most unusual conditions and it is only known that she once achieved 26.64 on a favourable

The launch of the *Ben-my-Chree* (III)

tide. Equally, it has been reported that after the outbreak of World War I she was loaded with ammunition and sent round the Cape to service warships that were under orders to sink the German cruiser *Konigsberg*. She is said to have made this long journey, including stops, at an overall speed of more than 22 knots. It is a good story, but no records have been traced in its support. The dates given in the surviving log notes on the ship at the Ministry of Defence suggest that she never had time to make such a journey between her first operations in the North Sea and her main war work in the Mediterranean. For her service in World War I see Chapter 5. In January 1917 she was bombarded and sunk by the Turks. She was refloated in 1920 and taken to Piraeus for breaking up. Her loss in action was keenly felt by the Manx people, who were intensely proud of her.

Ben-my-Chree (III)

29.   *Snaefell* (III).   No. 118606. Steel; twin-screw, built by Cammell Laird at Birkenhead in 1910 with engines and boilers also by Cammell Laird. Cost £59,275. Tonnage 1368; length 270′; beam 41′ 4″; depth 16′ 6″; speed 19 knots. Certified accommodation for 43 crew and 1241 passengers. Despite her modest size this dual purpose vessel was of some importance in the evolution of marine engineering in the Company's list. She was fitted with two sets of vertical 4-cylinder triple-expansion engines — the first of this type in the Company's ships. These developed a total i.h.p. of 5,300 and made her a very economical and useful ship. Designed for passenger and cargo work, she was put on the main winter service between Douglas and Liverpool. The ship was with the Steam Packet fleet for only four years. During the summer she worked from Douglas and Ramsey, usually on the Company's secondary routes. A popular ship, she was taken over and refitted as an armed patrol vessel at the outbreak of World War I. The work was done by Cammell Laird at Birkenhead, and she left the Mersey in Christmas week 1914 for an eventful war service with an unhappy ending. She was torpedoed and sunk in the Mediterranean on June 5, 1918.

Snaefell (III) KEIG

Tyrconnel MANX MUSEUM

30. *Tyrconnel.*   No. 99794. Single-screw steel steamship, built by J. Fullerton of Paisley in 1892 with their own engines and boilers. 274 tons; length 130′; beam 22′; depth 10′ 2″; two-cylinder compound engine; 450 i.h.p. Speed 9 knots. She was first registered in Glasgow in 1892, then in Londonderry in 1895. No record of the vessel remains in the Londonderry Custom's House, but she presumably traded from there until she was bought by the Manx Steam Trading Company of Castletown in 1902. She was acquired by the IOMSP in 1911 at a cost of £4,875, and worked the coastal trade until 1932, when she was sold to W. J. Ireland of Liverpool and eventually broken up at Danzig two years later. She was the first small cargo ship the Steam Packet had bought secondhand. She looked typical of her class of vessel, with funnel and machinery amidships. Her funnel could be described as off-white with black top and she was never changed to the Steam Packet's familiar black and red.

The Ramsey   MANX MUSEUM

31.   *The Ramsey*.   No. 104240. Steel built; twin-screw, reciprocating engines. Built in 1895 by the Naval Construction Company of Barrow-in-Furness, who also made the engines and boilers. 1443 tons; length 310' 2"; beam 37' 1"; depth 16' 4"; speed 19 knots; indicated horsepower 5,300. Certificate for 1162 passengers and 42 crew. This ship was originally the *Duke of Lancaster*, registered at Fleetwood and owned by the Lancashire and Yorkshire Railway, who operated her with the London & North Western on the Fleetwood-Belfast joint service. In March 1911 she was sold to an organisation called the Turkish Patriotic Committee, who renovated the engines and boilers, but the outbreak of the war between Italy and Turkey prevented the purchasers from taking delivery. The ship was then sold to the Steam Packet Company on July 12, 1912, with immediate change of name to *The Ramsey*. She was eventually known simply as the *Ramsey*, and she appears to have had an uneventful career in the Steam Packet fleet; but she survived only for the first year of World War I.

32.   *Peel Castle*.   No. 104233. Steel built; twin-screw. Built in 1894 by William Denny and Son, Dumbarton, with engines and boilers by the same yard. Tonnage 1474; length 310'; beam 37'; depth 16'; speed 17½ knots. Allowed 1162 passengers with crew of 42. She was powered by two reciprocating engines and developed 4100 i.h.p. This vessel was very similar to *The Ramsey*, although she had been built a year earlier. She was built for the Lancashire and Yorkshire Railway Company, registered at Fleetwood on May 15, 1894, and named *Duke of York*. She was sold to Turkish interests on March 23, 1911, having worked on the Fleetwood-Belfast run. The Steam Packet Company purchased the ship in similar conditions to the purchase of *The Ramsey*, but bought her a week later, on July 17, 1912, and changed her name immediately to *Peel Castle*. She served as an armed boarding vessel in World War I (see Chapter 5), returned to the Manx fleet, and was used on subsidiary and winter services. She was responsible for the direct Friday sailing from Liverpool to Ramsey, and also undertook excursion trips and cargo duties. In June 1924 she went ashore in Douglas Bay in a fog, but with no serious damage. She was broken up at Dalmuir on the Clyde in February, 1939.

Peel Castle

King Orry (III)   MANX MUSEUM

33.   *King Orry* (III).   No. 118608. Built in 1913 by Cammell Laird at Birkenhead with their engines and boilers. Steel ship with twin-screw geared turbines. Cost £96,000. Tonnage 1877; overall length 313'; beam 43'; depth 16' 11½"; speed 20¾ knots. Accommodation for 1,600 passengers and 59 crew. The last ship built for the Company before World War I. Here was another move forward in the marine engineering design of the Steam Packet steamers for she was the first of the Company's ships to be built with geared turbines. This gave her a low propeller speed while keeping a high turbine speed. Her twin screws were driven by two single-reduction geared turbine engines developing 9,400 i.h.p. She was another member of the fleet to have served in both World Wars. (See Chapters 5 and 7.) She had the distinction of following the light cruiser *Cardiff* in leading 21 German warships at the surrender of the German Grand Fleet at Scapa Flow in November 1918. Her most startling mishap in peacetime was her stranding near the Rock Lighthouse, New Brighton, while entering the Mersey on August 19, 1921. She was economical to run and could make 21 knots if necessary, and was extensively overhauled in 1934, then converted from coal to oil burning in 1939. She was bombed and sunk in the evacuation of Dunkirk on May 29, 1940.

34.   *Mona* (IV).   No. 124188. Steel built; twin-screw, fitted with two four-cylinder triple-expansion engines. Built for the Ardrossan-Portrush service for the Laird Line by Fairfields of Govan in 1907, and named the *Hazel*. Tonnage 1219; length 261'; beam 36'; depth 16'; speed 18 knots; indicated horsepower 3100. Accommodation for 58 crew; passenger complement 1,039 of whom 527 could be first class. The first of five vessels purchased by the Steam Packet Company in 1919 and 1920 to help make up the losses sustained by World War I. She was bought from G. and J. Burns of Glasgow on May 21, 1919, acting on behalf of the Laird Line, for £65,000. She had a maximum range of two full days steaming at an average fuel consumption of 66 tons of coal a day. She was placed mainly on secondary and night services and had an eventful career. In 1930 she ran ashore on the Conister Rock in Douglas Bay, an

Mona (IV)

accident that caused the outer face of Victoria Pier to be painted white to make it more distinctive. On another occasion she rammed the Crosby Light Vessel in a fog. For the last two years of her life she was mainly on reserve or cargo duty and was sold in December 1938 to E. G. Rees of Llanelly for scrapping.

Manxman (I)

35. *Manxman* (I). No. 118603. Steel ship; triple-screw turbine. Built by Vickers Sons and Maxim of Barrow-in-Furness in 1904 for the Midland Railway Company, used on the Heysham-Douglas service, and purchased from the Midland by the Admiralty in January 1915 during World War I. The Admiralty in turn sold her in March 1920 to the Steam Packet Company after the vessel had been released from requisition on Christmas Eve, 1919. Tonnage 2030; length 330'; beam 43'; depth 18'; speed 22 knots; 10,000 i.h.p. Boiler steam pressure 200 pounds p.s.i. Certificate for 2,020 passengers and crew of 80. She was no stranger to the Isle of Man and it was unnecessary to change her name. She was converted to an oil burner in 1921, and was the first Company ship to use oil fuel. She had seen war service as a seaplane carrier in World War I before she carried the Isle of Man Steam Packet flag, and she served during World War II. (See Chapters 5 and 7.) She never returned to the Company's service at the end of the war and her last duties were carried out ferrying service personnel and displaced persons between the Hook of Holland and Harwich. She was broken up at Preston in 1949.

Mona's Isle (IV)

36. *Mona's Isle* (IV). No. 120522. Steel; triple-screw turbine. Built in 1905 by William Denny at Dumbarton for the South Eastern and Chatham Railway Company and named *Onward*, and purchased from them by the Steam Packet Company in May 1920, the name being changed to *Mona's Isle* on August 27. Tonnage 1691; length 311' 2"; beam 40' 1"; depth 16' 6"; speed 22 knots; 7,500 i.h.p. Accommodation for 1479 passengers and 70 crew. She was said to be the only ship ever to carry the Manx flag down the Thames, for she was transferred to the Steam Packet Company when in Limehouse Docks of the Port of London. She was mainly used on summer work and was often on the routes to Dublin and Belfast. On Monday, June 29, 1936, she struck the Devil's Rock in Balscadden Bay, but was able to reach Dublin safely. She

was taking water and could not complete the return journey until repaired. In World War I she caught fire in Folkestone Harbour in October 1918. For her World War II service see Chapter 7. Returned to her owners after the war, worked for three years, and was broken up at Milford Haven in 1948.

37. *Snaefell* (IV).   No. 121331. Steel; triple-screw turbine. Built by Fairfield's at Govan in 1906, for G. and J. Burns, who used her on the Ardrossan-Belfast service. Purchased from Burns by the Steam Packet Company on March 22, 1920, for £160,000. Originally named *Viper* the name was changed to *Snaefell* on July 22, 1920 at Douglas. Tonnage 1713; length 315'; beam 39' 6"; depth 16' 6"; speed 21 knots; 6,500 i.h.p. Allowed 1700 passengers with a crew of 61. She served as a troopship in the English Channel in World War I and returned to Burns and the Belfast run until it was abandoned shortly after the war. In the Steam Packet Company's service she served at various times on most of their routes. In World War II (see Chapter 7) she was requisitioned and used mainly as a troopship, but after one year she was returned to the company and from 1940 she was one of the two passenger ships maintaining the wartime link with the mainland, first to Liverpool and then to Fleetwood. She was withdrawn from service in 1945 and sold for breaking up, but she was laid up at Port Glasgow for three years before being scrapped.

Snaefell (IV)

38. *Cushag*.   No. 124673. Steel; single-screw. Built by G. Brown & Co. at Greenock in 1908. Named *Ardnagrena* and first owned by James Waterson of Co. Antrim, who sold her to Humber Steam Coasters in 1914. Five years later she was sold once more, this time to a London broker, from whom the Steam Packet Company bought her in May, 1920, at a cost of £22,000. Her name was changed to *Cushag* on August 27, 1920. Tonnage 223; length 125'; beam 22' 1"; depth 9' 2"; speed 10 knots. One steam reciprocating engine: 350 i.h.p. Small and drawing so

Cushag   MANX MUSEUM

little water she was mostly used for cargo trade in the Island's smaller ports — Port St. Mary, Peel, Laxey and Castletown. After 20 years' work for the Company she was sold to London agents on January 26, 1943, and then went on to Stornoway on the Isle of Lewis for four years. She transferred to Kirkwall in the Orkneys in 1947, and her entry in the register ceases on July 20, 1957, when she was broken up at Grangemouth.

39.   *Manx Maid* (I).   No. 131763. Steel; triple-screw turbine. Built by Cammell Laird at Birkenhead in 1910 for the London and South Western Railway Co. who named her *Caesarea*, and employed her on the Southampton-Channel Islands service. Purchased from them by the Steam Packet Company in December 1923, for £9,000 and renamed *Manx Maid*, she

Manx Maid (I)

was refitted at a cost of £22,500 and converted to oil burning for £7,000, a total cost to the Steam Packet Company of £38,500. Tonnage 1504; length 284′ 6″; beam 39′ 1″; depth 15′ 8″; speed 20 knots. Accommodation for 1470 passengers and 51 crew. After being ashore near St. Helier in Jersey in 1923 she was refitted in Birkenhead and converted to oil fuel, having been bought by the Company while in the yards. She was powered by three directly coupled turbines and produced 6500 i.h.p. Her two boilers were doubled-ended circular return type with a working steam pressure of 160 pounds p.s.i. She was fired by six furnaces for each boiler and at 18 knots would consume 84 tons of oil in 24 hours — or 36 tons at 12 knots. In World War II (See Chapter 7) she became a "special duties" vessel and was returned to the Company after the War — without a main mast. She worked on peak traffic at week-ends for five more years until towed to Barrow for breaking up in November, 1950.

40.   *Ben-my-Chree* (IV).   No. 145304. Steel; twin-screw turbine. Built for the Company by Cammell Laird at Birkenhead in 1927. Her contracted cost was £185,000, but early construction work was held up by the long coal strike of 1926. Steel had to be bought from Continental sources at premium prices and the keel was not laid until November. The shipbuilders were granted extra payments to meet overtime costs, and promised a bonus of £2,000 if they met the delivery date of June 25, 1927. Eventually she was launched on April 5 and the trials were held on June 20. The builders met the deadline. In July Cammell Laird reported a direct loss of £17,000 on the building of the ship. The Steam Packet Company, very

Ben-my-Chree (IV)

satisfied with their new vessel, paid £192,000, including various extras and then agreed to round up the figure to £200,000 which remained the final cost to the company. Tonnage 2586; length 355'; beam 46'; depth 18' 6"; speed 22½-24½ knots. Certified space for 82 crew, and 2,586 passengers. The first ship to be built for the Company after the end of World War I, and the first to be built as an oil burner, fitted with two single-reduction geared turbines by Parsons, developing a total shaft horsepower of 10,300. Her working boiler pressure was 220 pounds p.s.i. During the thirties she was painted white with green below, an innovation in the Company's fleet. She had started her active service in the black paint that was traditional to the Steam Packet Company. The idea of changing her to white and green was decided on at a board meeting in April, 1932, when it was agreed that the move would have a definite advertising value when the vessel was in the Mersey. Vickers Armstrong did the work for £63. A fair estimate of the cost today would be £4,000. She was a fast and highly popular ship, with partially glass-enclosed decks. On normal service runs she was regularly recording averages of 20.75 knots between the Head and the Victoria Tower. Her average oil consumption per voyage on this route was 18.76 tons over five seasons. The ship had a varied World War II record. (See Chapter 7.) On returning to the Isle of Man after the War she needed very extensive overhaul. After long service she was eventually laid up in Birkenhead before being towed to Belgium for breaking up in December, 1965.

Victoria   MANX MUSEUM

41. *Victoria.*   No. 123811. Steel; triple-screw turbine. Built in 1907 by Wm. Denny at Dumbarton for the South Eastern and Chatham Railway who used her on the Dover-Calais service. Purchased from them by the Steam Packet Company in 1928 for £25,000, but with alterations, the total cost was £37,550. Passenger accommodation for 1,536; crew 41. Tonnage 1641; length 311'; beam 40' 1"; depth 16' 6"; speed 22 knots. Indicated horsepower 7500. Sister ship of the *Mona's Isle* (IV) - Fleet List number 36 - with a largely uneventful log. She was the last triple-screw direct drive turbine ship in the Company's fleet. Her turbines and propellers worked at 600 r.p.m., a rotation typical of the direct-drive turbine but much exceeding those used today with geared turbines. She was chartered by the L.M.S. for one day to assist in the

August Bank Holiday traffic on the Holyhead-Dun Laoghaire route in 1938. She made only one two-way crossing with 1,541 passengers in all, and the fee charged was £450. Her World War II service (see Chapter 7) included being mined in December 1940 but she was towed to safety and at the end of the war she returned to the Company's service. She was finally sold in January 1957 and broken up at Barrow.

42. *Ramsey Town*. No. 116015. Steel; twin-screw reciprocating. Built in 1904 by John Brown Ltd. of Clydebank for the Midland Railway's Heysham-Belfast service, registered at Belfast and named the *Antrim*. Purchased by the Steam Packet Company from the London, Midland and Scottish Railway group, of which the old Midland had become a part, in 1928. Cost including alterations £14,612. Tonnage 1954; length 330' 9"; beam 42' 2"; depth 17' 2"; speed 21 knots; 7870 i.h.p. One of the shortest records of service in the Steam Packet Fleet, being withdrawn in 1936. She was eventually scrapped at Preston in April, 1937.

Ramsey Town

43. *Rushen Castle*. No.109661. Steel; twin-screw; two triple-expansion reciprocating engines. Built at Barrow by Vickers, Sons and Maxim in 1898 for the Fleetwood-Belfast service run jointly by the Liverpool and Yorkshire and the London and North Western Railways. Originally named the *Duke of Cornwall* and registered at Fleetwood, she was bought by the Steam Packet Company from the L.M.S. Railway in 1928 for £29,254 including alterations, the second ship bought that year to service the Douglas-Heysham route from which the L.M.S. had withdrawn. Original accommodation for 1,052 passengers and 52 crew. Tonnage 1724; length 315'; beam 37' 1"; depth 16' 6"; speed 17½ knots; indicated horsepower 5520. Worked also on the winter service and stayed with the Company in World War II, being one of the ships that maintained the vital lifeline, first to Liverpool until the end of 1940 and then to Fleetwood. During the war she established what must have been a record for the longest modern passage between Liverpool and Douglas. On Saturday, January 27, 1940, she sailed for Douglas at 10.45, and was instructed by radio to make for Peel as an easterly gale had

blown up and made Douglas untenable. Being wartime the message named the captain but not the ship, and by mistake said "go to the East" instead of "go to the West", which would have indicated Peel to Captain Bridson. The captain duly tried to get into Douglas but was then signalled to make for Peel. By the time the ship got there the gale had veered and berthing at Peel was not possible. Eventually the *Rushen Castle* did get in at Peel — at 10.00 a.m. on Tuesday, January 30, after being at sea 71 hours. The Earl of Granville, Lieutenant Governor of the Island at the time was one of the passengers. She reopened the normal Douglas-Liverpool route on April 6, 1946, but was soon pulled out and laid up in Douglas. She was towed to Ghent for demolition in January, 1947.

Rushen Castle KEIG

44. *Peveril* (II). No. 145306. Steel; single-screw. Built by Cammell Laird at Birkenhead in 1929. Cost £42,600. The first cargo ship ordered directly by the Company, previous ones having been bought secondhand. Tonnage 798; length 205'; beam 34' 6"; depth 16'; speed 12 knots: powered by one triple-expansion directly coupled engine with boiler pressure at 200 pounds p.s.i. and developing 1250 i.h.p. Accommodation for 17 crew and 12 passengers. She traded mainly between Douglas, Ramsey and Liverpool for 35 years. With the arrival of her successor, *Peveril* (III), she became redundant and was sold to the Belton Shipping and Trading Company of London and was broken up at Glasson Dock, Lancaster, in May 1964. The *Peveril* had her name changed to *Peveril II* in October 1963 for the last few months of her life to release her original name for the new cargo vessel.

Peveril (II)   MANX MUSEUM

45.   *Lady of Mann* (I).   No. 145307. Steel; twin-screw geared-turbine. Built by Vickers
Armstrong at Barrow-in-Furness in 1930. Tonnage 3104; length 360'; beam 50'; depth 18' 6";
speed 23 knots. Certified for 2873 passengers and 81 crew. She cost £249,073. 1930 was the
Centenary year of the Company and the *Lady of Mann* was the largest ship ever built for it.
She was launched by the Duchess of Atholl, the Lady of Mann, after whom she was named.
She exceeded 22 knots on her trials but her speed was often over 23 knots on service. She was
driven by two sets of single-reduction geared turbines; steam pressure 220 pounds p.s.i., and
developed a shaft horsepower of 11,500. The ship was oil-fired by cylindrical scotch boilers.
Her hull was at first the Company's conventional black but was changed to white and green,
only to revert to black after World War II. Her initial work was on the Fleetwood service
where she took the place of the *Viking*. For her war service see Chapter 7. At the end of the
war she returned to the Manx fleet in 1946 after being reconditioned at Birkenhead. Her
career continued until August 1971 when she was sold to Arnott Young and Co. in Glasgow,
for breaking up.

The *Lady of Mann* was an exceedingly popular ship; when she came to be broken up
enthusiasts wrote in from all parts of Britain hoping to get souvenirs from her. Steam
Packet officials affectionately described her as having been "foreman built", for when she
was in the Vickers Armstrong yards at Barrow the builder was going through the very severe
slump that followed the 1929 crash on Wall Street. Most of the yard staff had been dismissed
and only key men kept on. It was these men who built the ship and a very fine one she proved.

Lady of Mann (I). Last sailing from Liverpool, 14th August, 1971.   K. P. LEWIS

46. *Conister*. No. 145470. Steel; single-screw, reciprocating engine. Built by the Goole Shipbuilding Company at Goole in 1921 with engines by C. and D. Holmes of Hull. Originally owned by G. T. Gilli and Blair (Cheviot Coasters Ltd.), Newcastle-upon-Tyne, and named *Abington*, who operated her from late November 1921. She was bought by the Company in January 1932, for £5,500, when her name was changed to *Conister*. Tonnage 411; length 145'; beam 24' 1"; depth 10' 9"; speed 10 knots. She was a single-hatch coaster and she survived World War II. (See Chapter 7.) She was the last coal-fired ship in the Company's fleet and the last using reciprocating triple-expansion engines, which developed 430 brake horsepower. She had two masts forward of the funnel and her machinery was aft. She was sold in 1965 to Arnott Young and Co. of Glasgow for scrapping.

Conister towed to the breakers

Mona's Queen (III)   MANX MUSEUM

47.   *Mona's Queen* (III).   No. 145308. Steel; twin-screw geared turbine. Built by Cammell Laird at Birkenhead in 1934. Cost £201,250. Tonnage 2756; length 337′; beam 48′; depth 17′; speed 22 knots. Certified for 2486 passengers and 83 crew. She was driven by two single-reduction geared turbines and produced 8500 brake horsepower; the first of the Company's ships to have water tube boilers, taking up less room than the scotch boilers previously used. She was an elegant ship, straight of stem and with elliptical stern. She was launched painted with a white hull over green. Her passenger accommodation was advanced for its day, with 20 cabins. Her life was brief as she was lost during the evacuation of Dunkirk on May 29, 1940.

48.   *Fenella* (II).   No. 145310. Steel; twin-screw geared turbine. Built by Vickers Armstrong at Barrow-in-Furness in 1937. Cost £203, 550. Tonnage 2376; length 314′ 6″; beam 46′; depth 18′; speed 21 knots. Crew accommodation for 68, and certificate for 1968 passengers. She was launched with her sister ship *Tynwald* (IV) from the Vickers' yard at Barrow on December 16, 1936. Both ships had water tube boilers with steam pressure of 250 pounds p.s.i., and two sets of single-reduction turbines, developing 8,500 brake horsepower. Smaller than their immediate predecessors they were designed especially for winter work and were the first ships of the Company to have cruiser sterns. Both ships worked on the heavy seasonal traffic on the main route, and both were much appreciated by passengers, especially in winter weather. The *Fenella* had possibly the shortest life of any ship in the Company's history, being sunk at Dunkirk on May 29, 1940. (See Chapter 7.) There is a disputed theory that she was raised by the Germans and later used by the Russians, but German naval documents refute this.

Fenella and *Tynwald* built in the thirties, lost during the Second World War.

Fenella (II) (left) and *Tynwald* (IV) two weeks before launching.

VICKERS-ARMSTRONG

Both vessels were launched at Barrow on 16th December, 1936.

Fenella (II)

49.   *Tynwald* (IV).   No. 165281. Steel; twin-screw turbine. Launched in December 1936 along with the *Fenella*, and entered the Steam Packet Company's service in June, 1937. Cost £203,550. Tonnage 2376; length 314′ 6″; beam 46′; depth 18′; speed 21 knots. Crew accommodation 68; 1968 passengers. Like her sister ship *Fenella* the target for the *Tynwald* was primarily the Liverpool-Douglas winter service. Unfortunately she lasted less than six years from her launching, being sunk by enemy action at Bougie, 150 miles East of Algiers, on November 12, 1942.

Tynwald (IV)   KEIG

King Orry (IV)   W. S. BASNETT

Aground in the Lune Estuary, January, 1976.   W. S. BASNETT

50. *King Orry* (IV). No. 165282. Steel; twin-screw geared turbine. Built by Cammell Laird at Birkenhead in 1946. Cost £402,095. Tonnage 2485; length 325'; beam 47'; depth 18'; speed 21 knots. Certificate for 2163 passengers and 68 crew. She was driven by two sets of Parsons turbines with single reduction gearing producing 8,500 brake horsepower. She had one funnel, a slightly raked stem, a cruiser stern and two pole masts. She adopted the system of prior booking of private cabins, which was considered to be a splendid innovation. She served for nearly 30 years in the Company's fleet, and made her last journey on August 30, 1975. She was bought by R. Taylor and Son of Bury for breaking up, having been berthed at Glasson Dock. She was alongside for more than two months and there were rumours that she might be resold to the Greeks. However, during a severe storm on the night of Friday, January 2, 1976, she broke away from her berth and drifted aground in the Lune Estuary. It was more than three months before she was refloated and Lynch and Son of Rochester, Kent, broke her up in 1979. Even then her name was to survive, for the breakers were approached by officials from the National Maritime Museum who purchased her starboard turbines, auxiliary machinery, a propeller and one of the three boilers. These were regarded as typical of the machinery used in the 1940's on cross-channel ships. On purchase the items were put into storage at Chatham Dockyard, the intention being to put them on display later at Greenwich. Meanwhile the *King Orry*'s machinery arrangement and specifications have been given to the Museum by the Company and the items have been added to the draughts collection at Greenwich.

Mona's Queen (IV) as *Barrow Queen.*

51. *Mona's Queen* (IV). No. 165283. Steel; twin-screw turbine. Built by Cammell Laird at Birkenhead and launched and delivered in 1946. Cost £411,241. Tonnage 2485; length 325'; beam 47'; depth 18'; speed 21 knots; i.h.p. 8500. Certified for 68 crew and 2163 passengers. Sister ship and substantially identical to the *King Orry* (IV). She worked for 16 years until her register was closed on October 22, 1962. Her ending came quickly as the Fleetwood berth had been declared unsafe at the time and no reconstruction was in sight. This made the *Mona's Queen* redundant and she was sold to the Chandris group of companies and was renamed four times. For the voyage to Greece she was named *Barrow Queen*, then in turn *Carissima, Carina* and *Fiesta*. She was adapted for cruising, with a tonnage of 3,158, a swimming pool, and accommodation for 340 passengers. She is not now believed to be in service.

52. *Tynwald* (V). No. 165284. Steel; twin-screw turbine, built by Cammell Laird at Birkenhead in 1947, and virtually identical with her two predecessors except for her tonnage, which is given as 2493. Cost £461,859. Her dimensions, speed and horsepower, also crew accommodation, matched the *Snaefell* and *Mona's Isle*. There was one accident in her history when she sank the barge *Eleanor* in the Mersey on February 25, 1952. She was popular and considered to have done a very sound job for the Company, and she continued to give service until 1974 when she was withdrawn from the fleet in August. By this time the newer car ferries in the Company were taking the bulk of the passenger traffic, and it was sound to reduce the number of passenger vessels from eight to seven. *Tynwald* was sold to John Cashmore of Newport, Mons. for £57,000, and resold to Spanish breakers who demolished her at Avtles in February 1975.

Tynwald (V)   W. S. BASNETT

53. *Snaefell* (V). No. 165287. Steel; twin-screw turbine. Built by Cammell Laird at Birkenhead in 1948 and started in the summer services that year. Cost £504,448. Tonnage 2489; but her dimensions, speed, horsepower and crew accommodation were otherwise similar to her three predecessors. She and *Mona's Isle* were the last ships on the Company's Heysham-Douglas service when it closed towards the end of August in 1974. Apart from an accident when she fouled her anchor off Llandudno in July 1976 and missed a sailing, she too had an efficient and uneventful career. But the predominance built up by the Steam Packet Company's car ferries in the 1970's made it sensible to withdraw another traditionally designed ship. She was thus sold to the Rochdale Metal Recovery Co. for scrap in 1978, and in the November was towed to Blyth for breaking up.

Snaefell (V)   W. S. BASNETT

Mona's Isle (V)   W. S. BASNETT

54. *Mona's Isle* (V). No. 165288. Steel; twin-screw turbine. Built by Cammell Laird at Birkenhead in 1951, to the dimensions, speed and horsepower of the previous four ships. Cost, £570,000. Her tonnage is 2495; with accommodation for 2268 passengers and 67 crew. She started service in March 1951 and was aground off Fleetwood after a collision with the *Ludo*, a small fishing vessel, on June 8, 1955. One man was lost from the *Ludo*, which was cut in half and sank almost immediately. On February 15, 1964 she went aground at Peel and had to be towed to Birkenhead for repairs. In August 1971 the *Mona's Isle* reopened the Fleetwood service from Douglas. She was the last of the Company's ships to use low pressure turbines.

Fenella (III)   W. S. BASNETT

55. *Fenella* (III). No. 165289. Steel; single-screw, diesel; built by Ailsa Shipbuilding Company at Troon in 1951. Cost £163,783. Tonnage 1019; length 210'; beam 37'; depth 16' 6"; speed 12½ knots. The Company's first motor ship and its first modern cargo vessel. She had a 7-cylinder British Polar engine of 1185 indicated horsepower. When the vessel was high and dry in port at low water the diesel generators were cooled by circulating water from the ballast tanks as though they were radiators. She carried cars, cattle and general cargo. She was sold after 22 years to the Greek owners, E. Mastichiades of Piraeus. Then, after some years in the Mediterranean, she caught fire and sank in 1978.

56. *Manxman* (II). No. 186349. Steel; twin-screw geared turbine. Built by Cammell Laird at Birkenhead in 1955. Cost £847,000. Tonnage 2495; length 325'; beam 46'; depth 18'; speed 21 knots. Certificate for 2393 passengers and 68 crew. Although outwardly very similar to the five previous post-war ships built for the Company by Cammell Laird she had a very different

engine room lay-out. Her two Pametrada turbines were driven by superheated steam at 350 pounds p.s.i. She was about the third ship ever built to use the Pametrada design, in which the turbine rotor turned at 4,300 r.p.m. Double reduction gearing was used to drive the two propellers at 270 r.p.m. She developed a normal shaft horsepower of 8,500.

Manxman (II)

W. S. BASNETT

57. *Manx Maid* (II). No. 186352. Steel; twin-screw geared-turbine. Built by Cammell Laird at Birkenhead in 1962. Tonnage 2724; length 325′; beam 50′; depth 18′; speed 21 knots; b.h.p. 9,500. Cost £1,087,000. Certified for 1400 passengers and crew of 60. To the engineer the ship is very similar to the *Manxman* except for Babcock and Wilcox integral furnace boilers, installed instead of the sectional header type. Her two double-reduction geared turbines develop a brake horsepower of 9,500. This ship has been a great success and is of major importance in the history of the Steam Packet Company for she is the first designed as a car ferry; she can take 90 cars. She is also the Company's first ship to be fitted with stabilisers. The design principle for vehicle loading is simple. A spiral set of ramps at the stern links with the car deck so that the vehicles can be driven on or off from the appropriate level on departure or arrival. This patented system of ramps facilitates loading and unloading at any state of the tide at any of the Company's ports. Cars have been carried to the Island for a number of years, but the tidal range at Douglas is considerable and it previously necessitated taking the vehicles on and off by crane, a slow and irksome process. The decision to build a new generation of car-ferrying vessels was taken in 1959 and *Manx Maid* was launched in January 1962. The design of the side loader with a spiral ramp at the stern is a unique feature of the Steam Packet Company's car ferries. In all, she was the 13th vessel that the Birkenhead yard had built for the Company since 1910. In 1979 she was fitted with a bow thruster mechanism, similar to that fitted to the *Ben-my-Chree* (V) the previous winter.

Manx Maid (II)   W. S. BASNETT

Peveril (III)   W. S. BASNETT

58.   *Peveril* (III).   No. 186353. Steel; single-screw motor vessel. Built by Ailsa Shipbuilding Company at Troon in 1964. Tonnage 1048; length 205'; beam 39'; depth 16' 6"; speed 12 knots. Cost £279,921. Fitted with 7-cylinder British Polar engine, direct-acting, developing 1400 brake horsepower. Accommodation for crew of 14. The second of the modern cargo ships to be built for the Company by the Ailsa yards. She was originally fitted with two 10-ton electric

cranes. She was converted to a container ship by her builders in 1972, when the cranes were removed and a cellular system for 56 standard units was installed.

59.   *Ramsey.*   No. 186354. Steel; single-screw motor vessel. Built by Ailsa Shipbuilding Company at Troon in 1965. Cost £158,647. Tonnage 446; length 149'; beam 28'; depth 12' 1'; speed 10 knots. Fitted with 6-cylinder British Polar engines developing 490 brake horsepower. Crew accommodation for 18. In the early 1970's containerisation resulted in a marked upsurge in freight business. In 1973 alone there was a 31 per cent rise in cargo. It was at first expected that the *Peveril* would handle all the new trade resulting from the container system and the *Fenella* (III) was sold at the beginning of the year. However, it became apparent that a second container vessel would be needed and to expedite matters one was chartered and later bought. The *Ramsey* was not suitable for conversion to take containers and at the end of 1973 she was sold to R. Lapthorn and Co. of Hoo, Rochester, Kent. She was renamed *Hoofort* and continues to trade around the south coast.

Ramsey   W. S. BASNETT

60.   *Ben-my-Chree* (V).   No. 186355. Steel; twin-screw turbine, built by Cammell Laird at Birkenhead, 1966. Cost £1,400,000. Tonnage 2762; length 325'; beam 50'; depth 18'; speed 21 knots. Accommodation for 1400 passengers; 60 crew. The machinery lay-out is similar to the *Manx Maid*, developing a brake horsepower of 9,500. In 1978 the ship was fitted with a bow thruster, driven by steam turbine of 500 horsepower. The second car ferry in the Company's fleet, and of interest as its last ship to be designed for two class passenger accommodation. She started her run in May 1966 and at the beginning of 1967 all the Company's ships, including the *Ben-my-Chree*, were converted to single class, the two class system having been employed for 136 years. In design and size she is virtually identical with the *Manx Maid*, built four years earlier in the same yards. The year 1966 when she started her operations was the year of the seamen's strike, which resulted in her being laid up for the first part of the summer. She made up for this to an extent by holding the Liverpool-Douglas route on her own for part of April 1975 when the *Mona's Queen* (V) was having her annual overhaul, and *Manx Maid* was enforced to be idle through an industrial dispute. Lovers of Manx ships were quick to appreciate that in 1978 the *Ben-my-Chree* was fitted with the ship's whistle from *Tynwald* (V), a traditional type organ whistle making a mighty reverberation.

Ben-my-Chree (V)   W. S. BASNETT

Mona's Queen (V)   W. S. BASNETT

61. *Mona's Queen* (V). No. 307621. Steel; twin-screw diesel. Built by Ailsa Shipbuilding Company at Troon in 1972 as the third of the side-loading car ferries. Cost £2,100,000. Tonnage 2998; length 322′; beam 52′; depth 17′ 6″; speed 21 knots. Accommodation for 1600 passengers, 55 crew, and approximately 100 vehicles. The first diesel passenger ship to be built for the Company. She was fitted with two 10-cylinder P.C.2 Crossley Pielstick engines, producing 10,000 brake horsepower, driving variable pitch propellers — the first time these have been used by the Company's fleet. Her speed and manoeuvering conditions can be controlled from the bridge or engine room by altering the pitch of the propellers. All engine conditions can be monitored from a specially-built control room inside the main engine room. Launched in Christmas week 1971 she came into the Company's service in June, 1972, just missing the peak traffic of the T.T. week. She is equipped with twin rudders, a 500 h.p. bow thruster unit, bow rudder and stabilizers. She has two inaugural voyages to her credit, making the first car ferry trip to Dublin in 1974, 133 years on from the first passenger service between the two ports and in June 1976 she made the first car ferry sailing from Fleetwood with 34 cars aboard.

Conister (II)   W. S. BASNETT

62. *Conister* (II). No. 187114. Steel; single-screw, diesel. Built by George Brown & Co., Greenock, in 1955, and registered in Liverpool as the *Brentfield*. She was sold to the Belfast Steamship Company in 1972, and renamed the *Spaniel*. She was chartered as a container ship by the Steam Packet Company in 1973, and then bought outright by them in November that year for £96,711, and renamed *Conister*. Tonnage 891; length 208'; beam 38'; depth 15'; speed 11 knots. She is driven by a 7-cylinder T.D.36 Sulzer engine, developing 1260 i.h.p. She has a capacity for 46 units.

Lady of Mann (II)   W. S. BASNETT

63. *Lady of Mann* (II). No. 359761. Steel; twin-screw diesel. Built 1976 by Ailsa Shipbuilding Company at Troon. Cost £3,800,000. The fourth and latest car ferry in the Company's fleet and the flag ship of the line. Tonnage 2990; length 322'; beam 52'; depth 17' 6"; speed 21 knots. Accommodation for 1600 passengers, and 61 crew. She is powered by two 12-cylinder diesel engines by Crossley Pielstick producing 11,500 brake horsepower. She is similar to the *Mona's Queen* (V) and can be regarded as a sister ship. She crossed from Douglas to Liverpool on June 30, 1976, on her maiden voyage, with 60 cars and 360 passengers. Through late delivery from the yards she was unlucky enough to miss the T.T. traffic of that year. She is the fastest of her contemporaries in the Steam Packet fleet, and could exceed her own performances but for the prudence exercised by all cross-channel shipping lines at a time of soaring fuel costs. This economy applies equally to the vessels on the various southern routes to the Continent. Yet on August 15, 1978, despite the necessity for fuel conservation, she crossed from Fleetwood to Douglas, *berth to berth,* in 2 hours 39 minutes, and to prove that this was no exception she did the same voyage the next day in 2 hours 40 minutes.

CHAPTER FOUR: *Engine Design*

M ARINE ENGINEERING HAS ADVANCED IN TWO ways. There are the great basic innovations such as the transition from paddle propulsion to propeller drive, the change from wood to iron in the ship's structure, the change from coal to oil, the arrival of the diesel, and so on. These big spectacular gains come piecemeal, maybe sometimes at long intervals. The less abrupt movement is in the refining of existing designs, the improvement of materials and their machining.

An example of this last development is the slow and deliberate raising of boiler pressure, where improved materials and manufacture steadily enabled pressure to be raised, thus increasing thermal efficiency.

The *Mona's Isle* (I), the Steam Packet Company's first vessel, produced steam at a pressure of 15 pounds per square inch. That, of course, was in 1830. The *Manx Maid* (II) and the *Ben-my-Chree* (V), which may well prove to be the last steam-driven ships to be built for the Company, had pressures of 350 pounds per square inch. That was in 1962 and 1966. It took more than 130 years to achieve a change of this magnitude.

Basic changes in engine design have been numerous. There could be argument as to what constituted a major development and what was merely a refinement. However, it is possible to pinpoint nine distinct and sometimes spectacular phases in the history of marine engineering as far as the Steam Packet Company is concerned.

These were as follows:
1. The side lever engine built into the Company's first vessel 150 years ago.
2. The oscillating engine, which had many advantages over the side lever.
3. The diagonal compound engine.
4. The single-screw vertical compound engine, which obviated the cumbersome and vulnerable paddle wheels.
5. The development of the twin-screw compound engine.
6. The triple-expansion twin-screw.
7. The direct driven triple-screw turbine which arrived with the *Viking*, the first turbine steamer in this category to be built for the Company
8. The geared turbines introduced in the *King Orry* (III), built by Cammell Laird before the Great War of 1914. This became the standard passenger ship engine design in the Company's fleet up to and including the *Ben-my-Chree* (V) in 1966, excluding cargo vessels and some second-hand ships bought to replace war losses.
9. The latest of the major developments, namely the diesel-driven motor vessel.

Brief details of the various engines appear in the previous chapter under the entries for the individual ships. In this chapter the concern is for the overall pattern of progress rather than for the ships that pioneered forward movements in design.

KING ORRY 1842

Side elevation drawing by A. M. Goodwyn of a Napier side lever marine engine as fitted to the *King Orry*, 1842.

In some categories the Company has been among the leaders in the shipping world. This was certainly the case with the side lever engine with which the Company started its long career. The *Mona's Isle* (I) was one of the earliest examples of Robert Napier's work and he was rightly and understandably proud of it, maintaining in later life that a large part of his prosperity was based on the success of this small vessel. The *Mona's Isle* was probably the most efficient steamship of its day, and partly because of this, the side lever engine became the most popular type for marine purposes. It was used for driving ocean-going ships until the early 1850's when the oscillating engine was being introduced.

The Steam Packet Company first adopted the oscillating engine in 1860, when Tod and Macgregor built *Mona's Isle* (II). The two cylinder engine of this type was adopted for the three paddlers, *Snaefell* (I), *Douglas* (II), and *Tynwald* (II), all built by Caird of Greenock between 1863 and 1866.

The diagonal compound engine followed and was used intermittently for a number of years. In the Steam Packet fleet the main examples of this type were fast paddlers *Queen Victoria*, *Prince of Wales* and *Mona* (III). The high pressure cylinder was placed horizontally in the engine with the low pressure diagonally to the centre of the shaft. Several other companies copied the design for cross-Channel steamers and the Steam Packet Company later adopted this design in the *Empress Queen*, an oustanding ship.

An even more important development was the single-screw vertical compound engine represented firstly by the *Mona* (II), built by Laird in 1878, the first single-screw steamer in the Company's fleet list. She was fitted with a set of vertical compound engines, which were more economical to run than their predecessors, and the screw drive was superior to the paddle particularly on the winter service.

Even so the paddle steamer was far from obsolete. The *Mona's Queen* (II), built by Barrow Shipbuilding, was ordered in 1885 and the *Mona's Isle* (III) had been built by Caird's in 1882. The *Empress Queen* was another paddler, built as late as 1897, while *Mona* (III), the last paddle ship to join the Company's fleet, was bought from a defeated rival as late as 1903. So the paddle drive took years before it disappeared from the Company's service, the last paddler being the *Mona's Queen* (II), which was not disposed of until 1929. Even then there were many paddlers on station in British coastal fleets. The Isle of Wight was served by them throughout World War 2, and small paddlers continued to ply on the Clyde, in the Bristol Channel and elsewhere, until comparatively recently.

Mona (II) testified that the vertical compound engine was more economical in space and performance than its forerunners. As a result the ship's basic design was followed when in 1881 Barrow Shipbuilding produced the *Fenella* (I), one of the very earliest twin-screw vertical compound steamers. Her two sets of vertical compounds gave her an i.h.p. of 1200 and a speed of 13½ knots. This did not make her the fastest or most powerful of the Steam Packet vessels to date and many of her predecessors were substantially larger than she was. Up to that time the *King Orry* (II) at 1,104 tons, 4,000 i.h.p. and 17 knots was the star of the fleet. But the *Fenella* (I) had a boiler pressure of 85 pounds per square inch and she proved that greater economy was now to be had by using higher steam pressures with compound engines producing a higher piston speed than would have been practical in a paddle steamer.

It was observed by the late J. B. Waddington, a director of the Steam Packet Company and J. R. Kelly, its Superintendent Engineer in 1930, that the whole world of marine engineering was pressing forward at the time the *Fenella* (I) was built. This screw-driven steamer with her vertical compounds working from a higher pressure level created an altogether new and successful concept in ship building. The *Fenella* herself survived the First World War and was in continuous service for 48 years; her record was significant.

As far as the Steam Packet Company was concerned the paddle steamer was further improved rather than discarded. *Mona's Isle* (III), built in 1882, was fitted with compound oscillating cylinder engines, working at a boiler pressure of 90 pounds per square inch. *Mona's Queen* (II), also a paddler, was built by the Barrow company in 1885, with two sets of compound oscillating cylinder engines giving a combined i.h.p. of 5,000, the highest power output in the first 29 ships in the Steam Packet fleet. She also had the highest speed—18 knots—to date. Three more paddlers came on the scene and quickly exceeded her performance records. The *Prince of Wales* and *Queen Victoria* were built by Fairfield in 1887 and purchased from the Isle of Man, Liverpool and Manchester Steamship Company in 1888. Both were capable of 20½ knots, and had an i.h.p. of 6,500. Their boiler steam pressure was 110 pounds per square inch. They had coupled two crankshaft compound engines, for a brief description of which see pages 31 - 32. Within two years Fairfield had beaten their own previous best in the building of paddlers, with the Steam Packet's *Empress Queen*, with her i.h.p. of 10,000 and a speed of 21½ knots. She was the last paddle ship to be built for the Company and had some claim to be the fastest paddle driven cross-Channel steamer ever built. Boiler steam pressure had by then risen to 140 pounds per square inch. She was driven by engines of the diagonal three-crank compound type having a h.p. cylinder in the centre with two l.p. cylinders, one on each side.

However, a much greater step forward was taken in 1905 when the triple-expansion twin-screw engine arrived with *Tynwald* (III). She was a substantially smaller vessel than her contemporary paddlers and was one of many ships that incorporated the triple-expansion

Engines of the paddle steamer, *Empress Queen*.

Manoeuvering platform of *Viking*.   W. PARRY

Engine room platform of *Ben-my-Chree* (III)   VICKERS

Engine room of *Manxman* (I)   VICKERS

design to be built for several companies between 1891 and 1904. Her two boilers produced steam pressure of 160 pounds per square inch.

An even more dramatic development came in 1905 when Armstrong Whitworth produced the remarkable *Viking*, the first turbine-driven ship in the Steam Packet fleet. She was triple-screwed, powered by three sets of directly-driven turbines. Her working speed approached 23 knots and at times she made 24. Three years later the Company again chose directly-driven turbines for the *Ben-my-Chree* (III), built by Vickers, Sons and Maxim. In this vessel the boiler pressure rose to 170 pounds per square inch, continuing the steady increase made possible by improving engineering and material standards and thereby securing greater thermal efficiency.

The next marine engine development by the Company occurred in 1913 with the arrival of the *King Orry* (III), built by Cammell Laird at Birkenhead. She was the first geared turbine steamer in the Company's fleet. The engines were single-reduction geared, driving twin screws. With the exception of some of the ships bought to replace war losses and some cargo vessels, the twin-screw geared turbine became the standard engine design of the fleet until 1972, the year of its first passenger motor vessel.

The gearing gave the *King Orry* a propeller speed of some 270 r.p.m., and the gear made it possible for a high turbine speed to be maintained. Here again was a steady improvement in thermal efficiency. Direct drive turbine ships, particularly with triple-screws, had a much higher propeller speed, often 600 r.p.m.; this had meant a poorer thermal efficiency than in the new gearing design. The practice today on Steam Packet diesel vessels is to have a constant propeller speed of 275 r.p.m., with the ship's speed controlled by variations of propeller pitch.

Engine room of *Mona's Isle* (V)   W.S. BASNETT

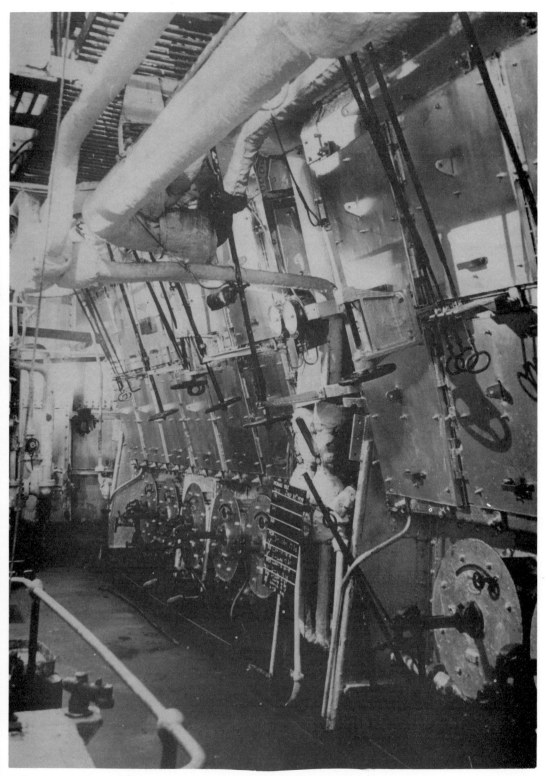

Boiler room of *Mona's Isle* (V) W.S. BASNETT

Engine room manoeuvering platform of *Ben-my-Chree* (V)   W.S. BASNETT

Boiler room of *Ben-my-Chree* (V)

W.S. BASNETT

Engine Control room, *Lady of Mann* (II). W. S. BASNETT

The diesel motor ship became the latest important mechanical development in the Company's fleet; the twin-screw geared turbine design had lasted for many years. When they appeared, however, the diesels had economic advantages over any type of steam driven engine and but for the abnormal fuel cost position that has arisen since the revolution in Iran, they could be expected to be standard usage in cross-Channel ships for many years to come.

Some of the largest units in the international mercantile fleet, including the heaviest oil tankers, are running most successfully with diesel engines. This situation, however, could change rapidly. The cost of oil fuel has been rising alarmingly and at the time of writing the increased costs show no sign of moderating. If the situation deteriorates in the next few years it could be that ship designers will be driven to consider new methods of producing power.

A return to raw coal burner is perhaps unlikely. But coal is, of all sources of energy, the most readily available. Experiments are known to be going on to make what the scientists are

Starboard engine, *Lady of Mann* (II).

W. S. BASNETT

already calling a fluidised bed — that is a surface containing a catalyst that will become molten when coal or some other combustible is sprayed on it. The resultant heat can produce steam or gas to drive a turbine. These methods could be regarded as the latest refinement in coal burning and are still in the experimental stage. There may yet be an urgent need for them. Other propellants could be liquid gas, which once again could be used for driving turbines or internal combustion engines. Nuclear power could also be applied for the steam generation. This last is extremely unlikely in coastal ships in the forseeable future, however, owing to the costs involved.

The possibilities develop into an almost Wellsian future. While oil fuel costs continue to rise, alternative sources of energy have to be investigated with urgency. Meanwhile, the diesel motor vessel remains the latest in the long line of engine developments that stretches back to Napier's side lever engine in 1830.

CHAPTER FIVE: *The Great War: 1914-18*

THE IMMEDIATE EFFECT ON THE STEAM PACKET
Company of the start of the Great War of 1914–1918 was simple and mundane. It began in
what was, or should have been, the peak of the holiday season. Traffic should have been
booming. Instead the Directors convened a special meeting on August 10, only a few days
after the outbreak, to consider the sudden change in the position. The passenger arrivals over
the previous week-end had fallen to a most serious extent.

It was at once decided that the *Ben-my-Chree*, the *Viking*, and the *Empress Queen* should be
taken out of service as soon as possible, and that while the main route from Liverpool must
continue various minor routes should be withdrawn.

Within a week the service from Whitehaven was suspended.

For the next two months the Company and the Manx people continued at their business,
although steadily contracting their normal summer activities. The war front was as yet far
away; the great mass of khaki had yet to move. The tramping columns of prisoners of war
were in the future.

Yet the sea war, which was in many ways the more immediate to the Manx, soon became a
reality. By the end of October the *King Orry*, the *Peel Castle* and *The Ramsey* had been
requisitioned by the Admiralty and had left Manx waters, followed shortly by the *Snaefell*. By
January, 1915, the *Ben-my-Chree*, that remarkable ship, had been requisitioned, and the Royal
Navy had asked for particulars and plans of all the Company's paddle steamers.

Soon the *Queen Victoria* and the *Prince of Wales* had also been commandeered and were away
in Barrow, being fitted out by Vickers.

Soon, too, came the realisation that German submarines were prowling in the Irish Sea.
The war had come up with the tide. In vain the officials of the Steam Packet Company pleaded
that so many ships had been requisitioned that they could now barely maintain the vital
lifeline, the mail, goods and passenger service with the mainland; no further tonnage could be
spared for the Admiralty.

The *Empress Queen* was then added to the list within a week and ordered to proceed to
Southampton for national service.

So from 15 vessels at the declaration of war the Steam Packet fleet was reduced to four
within a few months; 11 had been chartered or purchased by the Admiralty, to be fitted out
and armed for specialised work.

Of the 11 only four returned to the Company four years or more later, when the war was
over and won. The *King Orry*, the *Mona's Queen* and the *Peel Castle* came back. The *Viking* was
repurchased by the Company in 1919. Three ships were retained by the Government.

Four were lost. *The Ramsey* went first, a year after the war started; the *Empress Queen* went
aground while troop carrying in 1916; the spectacular *Ben-my-Chree* was bombarded and sunk
in 1917, and the *Snaefell* was torpedoed in the Mediterranean in June, 1918.

The Manx fleet at the start of the war was not unreasonably regarded by its owners as the finest cross-channel fleet in the world. Now four of its more modest vessels were to stay on the home service, and the fast ships were to go off troop carrying, for which they would seem ideal on the run to France from ports in the south of England.

Such was the feeling. In practice it did not work out like that.

Two of the 11 ships became seaplane carriers and played a most notable part in the development of naval aviation. Only two of the remaining nine were used solely as troopers; the others were fitted out as anti-submarine net-layers, armed boarding vessels, or used for general fleet purposes, sometimes far off. One, the *King Orry*, although fitted out for boarding parties, was even attached to the British Grand Fleet and worked out of Scapa Flow.

* * *

The record of the *Snaefell* (III) is typical of the work of the Steam Packet Company's ships in World War I. She seems to have been the first of the fleet to go off on active service and in all she saw nearly four years of very active service indeed.

On being chartered by the Admiralty she was sent to Cammell Laird's in Birkenhead, her original builders, and was fitted with armament and given necessary alterations. She sailed for Plymouth on December 18, 1914, modestly armed with two 12-pounders and one anti-aircraft gun and manned by a crew of 105.

She became one of the four coastal steamers in the Plymouth Patrol, and had a reasonably uneventful introduction to war, steaming from Start Point to Land's End and then to a position in mid-Channel, on the other side of which the French Navy took over the patrol. Her duty was to intercept all shipping and issue any necessary instructions covering the likely position of enemy submarines and such matters. It meant four days at sea and two days in port, a very different weekly régime from what was in store for her crew.

In the following April the *Snaefell* had a minor brush with a German submarine but failed to find her target although given the chance of a shot at what seemed to have been close range. Two months later she was away to more desperate matters, escorting the monitor *Raglan* to Gallipoli. Once at the Dardanelles she worked in the monitor's squadron, even carrying seaplanes which were sent up as artillery spotters for the *Raglan*'s gunners.

It was an eventful summer for the Manx ship. She was soon based at Mudros, on Lemnos, some 60 miles from the Dardanelles. From the island she carried troops and stores to the

Snaefell (III) on war service

IMPERIAL WAR MUSEUM

combat area in Suvla Bay. Early in August she was damaged by shellfire. She was then switched to shore patrol work, closely watching Turkish movements. During this time she went aground and was holed. After emergency repairs she eventually reached Alexandria, where she was made shipshape once more and was back on active duties in about six weeks, patrolling the Bulgarian coast. This work entailed danger from floating mines, shore batteries, and Bulgarian aircraft, against which the *Snaefell* at first had no defence.

During this phase of her work she was holed by a six-inch shell from a Turkish battery but once more she was lucky.

Then followed the evacuation from Gallipoli after which the ship was given troop-carrying duties for several months, on one occasion being heavily shelled by a submarine when laden with Turkish prisoners of war who had been taken aboard in Cyprus. She escaped in the darkness.

She was refitted at Alexandria in the spring of 1918 and after being held up by a serious fire that broke out aboard while she was in harbour she was able to leave for Malta early in June. She never arrived for she was torpedoed and sunk on June 5 with the loss of three lives.

*   *   *

The *Peel Castle* had an entirely different war. She was chartered by the Admiralty as soon as the Manx summer season traffic had returned home and spent five weeks at Birkenhead being fitted out by Cammell Laird's. She was to have 100 officers and crew and was fitted up as an auxiliary, capable of carrying boarding parties and prize crews. She was put under the command of an R.N.R. officer who had spent years with the P. and O.

She sailed under the White Ensign in January, 1915, her engine room manned mostly by Steam Packet Company personnel, and became part of the Downs Boarding Flotilla, a section of the Dover Patrol. She remained on this work for three years and a month.

The life was routine, ten days at sea and four in port at Dover. The duties were plain; to regulate the heavy maritime traffic between the Kent coast and the Goodwin Sands, to act as one of the guard ships; to halt and examine all neutral shipping proceeding to Continental ports; to search for enemies, and to seize cargo intended for them.

The work was heavy; the Dover Straits were closed by anti-submarine nets and minefields. No ship could pass except through the Patrol, and at one time the British vessels were intercepting, searching and marshalling up to 115 vessels a day.

In this strenuous work the *Peel Castle* played a busy and successful part. She first saw action from the guns of a retreating merchantman, and then at least once from the guns of British shore batteries. She was under bombardment in the many air raids; she sent boarding parties on to many ships. Her crew made a number of captures of enemy personnel who were trying to get back to Europe hidden in neutral ships. She even scored the important capture of an agent for Admiral Tirpitz.

On too many occasions the ship had to pick up survivors from vessels that had been victims of marauding submarines.

In 1916 she was very badly damaged by fire and had to be refitted at Chatham. Later she was transferred to the Orkneys where, having been fitted with depth charge throwers and paravanes and with her boat deck extended as a landing for kite balloons, she patrolled north of the Shetlands.

The *Peel Castle* was next moved to the Humber-Tyne Patrol, an area where shipping was very concentrated and where losses had been heavy. With her observer aloft in the balloon she would cruise up and down outside the convoys, spotting submarines.

The war over, she was refitted once more, this time as a troop carrier, work she continued until May, 1919, after which she returned to Liverpool and was made shipshape to resume her peacetime Steam Packet Company duties.

*   *   *

The third of the first group of the Company's ships to be called up was *The Ramsey*. Her career in the War was to be short; she survived less than a year.

She finished her 1914 season from Douglas to Liverpool and was fitted out as an armed boarding vessel by Cammell Laird's, with two 12-pounder guns and a crew of 98. She was based in Scapa Flow and her work consisted of night patrols. She was usually accompanying two destroyers, but not always. It was dangerous work, directed by radio from headquarters, and carried out without navigation lights and with manned guns throughout.

In the course of a few months *The Ramsey* intercepted and challenged many ships, sometimes putting a prize crew aboard and taking the suspect into port.

On her last patrol she had steamed for 12 hours when after dawn on August 8, 1915, she saw smoke over the horizon, gave chase, and came down on a large tramp steamer flying the Russian flag. She ordered her to stop. All seemed in order.

The Ramsey proceeded alongside the vessel, which had duly stopped. The suspect then hoisted the German flag, and fired at what amouted to pointblank range. The broadside killed the Commander and the officers on the bridge of *The Ramsey*. At the same time the raider, the German *Metior*, fired a torpedo shattering *The Ramsey*'s stern.

Fifty-two of *The Ramsey*'s crew were killed; 46 were picked up by the raider, which in peacetime had been the *Vienna*, trading between Hamburg and Leith. *The Ramsey* went down in four minutes.

*   *   *

Perhaps it is not surprising that the *Ben-my-Chree* (III) had the most spectacular war record of all the Steam Packet Company's ships, for she was the flagship of its fleet when war broke out, and was quite the outstanding channel steamer of her time. She carried more passengers than any other of the Company's vessels and was faster and much more powerful. No cross-Channel steamer of her day could rival her speed.

The Steam Packet directors recorded that she had been requisitioned at their first meeting in January, 1915, and she had, in fact, been ordered to report on January 2. The Cammell Laird yards then took her over and she was converted into a seaplane carrier at Birkenhead. She was soon to contribute to the development of naval aviation.

Ten former cross-channel steamers from various sources were chosen by the Admiralty to carry seaplanes. Their speed was the determining consideration. They had to be able to hold station if operating with the Grand Fleet. Two of the ten were Steam Packet Company ships — the *Ben-my-Chree*, and the *Viking*, which the Royal Navy renamed the *Vindex*. A third ship was the *Manxman*, built for the Midland Railway Company and used on its Heysham-Douglas run, and then purchased by the Steam Packet Company when the war was over.

The *Ben-my-Chree*, in common with the others, was fitted with a large and inelegant aircraft hangar aft, a smaller one forward, and a flying off platform, also forward, of about 60 feet in length. Cranes were also fitted for hoisting the seaplanes aboard from the water. This new superstructure was on three levels and was a sizeable job, for the large hangar was built across the entire width of the ship and could house four seaplanes. A well-equipped workshop for servicing the aircraft was fitted up in the deck below the main hangar.

The ship was commissioned on March 3, 1915, and her first base was Harwich, where she arrived on April 28. She was armed with four 12-pounders and four anti-aircraft guns. She carried four Short 184 seaplanes whose wing span was 63½ feet and length 40 feet. They were powered by Sunbeam 225 h.p. engines and carried radio and a crew of two. Their armament consisted of one Lewis gun in the rear cockpit and they could carry a 14-inch torpedo or 520 pounds of bombs. At an altitude of 2,000 feet the flight speed was 88 m.p.h. Flight time was limited to two hours, 45 minutes. The Swordfish in the early part of World War II did a somewhat similar job and was not all that faster.

When the *Ben* was fitted up as a carrier it was assumed that the Short 184's could get airborne using the tilted forward trackway. In practice their weight was against them; they needed a longer run so they had to be winched and lowered to the sea, just as they had to be lifted from it. This meant that the ship had to be almost stationary, a serious problem in action.

During 1915, when she was first in action, the *Ben* also carried Sopwith Schneider floatplane fighters to intercept Zeppelins over the North Sea. These were single-seater biplanes, made of wood and fabric covered, powered by 100 h.p. Gnome Monosoupage engines and with a span of 25' 8" and a length of 22' 10". They were 10 feet in height and armed with one Lewis gun and one 65 pound bomb. These, too, were difficult to get airborne when lowered into the sea. To overcome this problem two-wheeled dollies were fitted beneath the floats, hoping that these aircraft could then operate from the short flying-off deck, which had already proved unsatisfactory in the case of the heavier Short 184's. Experiments were carried out on another converted merchantman, the Cunarder *Campania*.

The device worked. The first successful take off is recorded on August 6, 1915, the pilot being Flt. Lt. W. L. Welsh.

By August, however, the *Ben-my-Chree* was away in the Mediterranean. She reached Malta on June 7 and started her active service in support of the Gallipoli campaign by steaming east the following day. She was soon in action spotting for naval gunners in bombardments of Turkish positions. She remained actively on the station until the evacuation of Gallipoli, when she was said to have been the last British ship to have pulled out after the military stores had been burned.

Her place in naval aviation history was gained on August 12, 1915, when one of her Short 184's spotted a 5,000 ton Turkish supply ship and attacked her from the air. The aircraft was piloted by Flt. Commander C. H. Edmonds, R.N.A.S., and he aimed a 14-inch Whitehead torpedo at his target at a range of 890 feet, having glided down to 15 feet from the water. The vessel was hit amidships and sunk. It was the first successful attack against a ship with a torpedo dropped from the air and as such has a niche in the *Guinness History of Air Warfare*.

The record is contested. A British submarine claimed to have torpedoed the same Turkish ship just before the seaplane arrived. Yet Commander Edmonds had seen his torpedo strike the vessel after he had attacked and had started his climb; there seems little reason to doubt him. He had been hoisted out from the *Ben* at first light, the torpedo had been slung under his aircraft, he had lifted the heavily-loaded plane after a short run, and had headed north to where the Turkish ship had been reported. Flying north at 800 feet he is said to have sighted his quarry, cut his engine and dropped down. The claim seems fair enough.

In any case, the *Ben-my-Chree* can rest with distinction on the facts of its further conquests. For five days after this sinking two more torpedo attacks were launched against Turkish supply ships and both came from the *Ben*. Two seaplanes made a sortie; Commander Edmonds was in one, hit a Turk and set her on fire. Flt. Lieut. G. B. Dacre was in the second; his machine developed engine trouble and he landed in the sea. However, seeing an enemy tug he was able to taxi towards it, score a direct hit from close range, and turn away. His load now lightened, he picked up power, took off, and flew back to the carrier.

Ben-my-Chree (III) at Mudros in November 1915   IMPERIAL WAR MUSEUM

Three weeks later the *Ben-my-Chree* was in a very different type of action. She received an S.O.S. signal from the troopship *Southland* as she was sinking; she arrived on the scene in time to rescue 815 men who had taken to crowded lifeboats and rafts. They included 694 Australians and New Zealanders and 121 crew.

The *Ben* had a busy war in the eastern Mediterranean, bombing raids into Bulgaria and spotting for naval monitors. As 1916 ended she went through the Suez Canal to the Red Sea, where she bombarded Arab camps and bombed railways. She then returned and resumed her normal duties. Her end came on January 11, 1917. She was anchored off the island of Castellorizo, which was about two miles from the coast and occupied by the French. Severe

Ben-my-Chree (III) sunk off Castellorizo   MANX MUSEUM

winds had prevented her aircraft from flying and unknown to the *Ben* a Turkish battery had taken up position on the mainland opposite. It opened up at the seaplane carrier, demolishing the large hangar, holing the petrol store, and setting the ship alight. As the steering gear had been shot away it was impossible to move out of range. The ship was abandoned after half an hour. One of *Ben's* three motor-boats was still unharmed, and using the ship itself as a shield the crew of 250 were able to get safely ashore. There were only four wounded. Commander Samson and the Chief Engineer were the last men to leave the ship, which was shelled for five hours until it settled down as a burned out wreck in shallow water.

Accompanied by three of the crew the two officers later returned and removed the breech-blocks from the guns, and saved the ship's cat and two dogs.

* * *

The *Viking* was requisitioned on March 23, 1915, fitted out and commissioned at Liverpool on August 11. She was renamed the *Vindex* by the Admiralty, who purchased her on the following October 11. She had been converted to a seaplane carrier in similar fashion to the *Ben-my-Chree* and she first served at the Nore and at Harwich before proceeding to the Mediterranean.

She carried four Short 184 seaplanes and could carry up to four single-seater Bristol Scout fighters, which were powered by 80 h.p. Gnome engines. These were landplanes on wheels. At the end of a mission they had to ditch and remain supported by floatation bags until they could be lifted back aboard by crane.

The *Vindex* was attached to the Grand Fleet at Harwich in November, 1915, and on November 5, after a month of experiments mainly at sea, she, too, claimed her place in the history of air warfare. One of her fighter aircraft was finally launched from her flying off platform, soon to be called the flight deck. *This was the first instance of a land plane with a wheeled undercarriage taking off from the deck of an aircraft carrier.* The pilot was Sub. Lieut. H. F. Towler. The achievement is in the naval air records.

The light plane carried armament consisting of 48 Ranken Darts, which could be released in groups of three and which would explode on contact with Zeppelins.

The breakthrough having been achieved, Bristol Scouts were soon taking off regularly from the short platform of these small aircraft carriers.

Viking (renamed *Vindex*) in World War I   IMPERIAL WAR MUSEUM

In 1916 the *Vindex* conducted more flying experiments at sea and again they were successful. She carried Sopwith 1½-Strutter fighters that had been fitted with skids instead of wheels. Using these skids as slides the planes were able to fly off from the carrier's forward trackway, which was only about 64 feet long. This was the first British aircraft that was fitted with synchronising gear, enabling the pilot to fire a fixed front gun through the arc of the propeller.

After strenuous work with the Harwich and other North Sea forces the *Vindex* went to the Eastern Mediterranean in 1918, where she did work similar to the *Ben-my-Chree*. She operated there until the end of the War and returned to Plymouth in March, 1919.

The Steam Packet Company bought her back from the Admiralty a month later. She served throughout the twenties and thirties, survived war service once again and after a further period with the Company was sold for breaking up in 1954.

*　*　*

The *Empress Queen* was chartered by the Admiralty on February 6, 1915. She was ideally suited as a troop carrier, and it took only a fortnight to fit her out at Barrow. She then went to Southampton and two days later was on the first of her wartime duties, taking 1900 men of a Scottish regiment to Le Havre. She made crossing after crossing, and when homeward bound would bring back "liberty men", many of whom had been only a short journey back from the trenches.

Her end was unexpected. She had been regarded by the authorities as an exceptionally reliable paddle steamer; she had never stopped for weather or engine trouble.

Then on February 1, 1916, she was returning to Southampton from Le Havre with 1,300 men who were going on leave. The weather was foul, the visability was but a few yards, when she ran ashore at five in the morning on the Ring Rocks off Bembridge, Isle of Wight. The rocks are a quarter of a mile out from the cliffs, they were flat, and she ran well up on to them on a rising tide. The wind was light, the sea was calm.

Destroyers took off the troops, the crew remaining on board as efforts were made to pull the vessel off. It was not expected to be a difficult task, but it proved impossible. The weather changed in a matter of hours and a gale blew up.

The crew was then taken to safety over the rocks at low tide. The *Empress Queen*, regarded as the fastest paddle steamer of her day when Fairfield's built her in 1897, was broken up by wind and tide as the seasons passed.

She became a familiar landmark to Southampton and Portsmouth shipping. Her two funnels were still to be seen above the water on Armistice Day. During the following summer, after a long and heavy gale, they finally disappeared.

*　*　*

The *Mona's Isle* (III) was sold to the Admiralty in 1915 and did not return to the Company's fleet at the end of the war. She was fitted out by Vickers in September, 1915, as a net-laying ship for anti-submarine work.

She was usually stationed at Harwich and did very varied work, quite apart from net-laying. Perhaps her most noteworthy mission was to the wreck of a Dutch steamer that had been torpedoed and sunk beyond the Cork lightship off the southern Irish coast. It was known that the Dutchman had been carrying bullion, and the net-layer acted as base ship for the salvaging operations.

Gold valued at £86,000 was recovered, after which the paddle steamer made a fast getaway from an area where German submarines were particularly menacing.

The *Mona's Isle* had a number of varied missions; she patrolled the west coast of Ireland, she assisted in rescue work from a sinking warship and she searched for survivors from two British submarines that had been lost.

* * *

The First World War history of the *Mona's Isle* would not have been dissimilar to that of the many paddle-steamers pressed into service during the great emergency. The *Mona's Queen* (II) had one experience that made her story different.

She was chartered in 1915 and was used as a troop carrier mainly between Southampton and Le Havre. The work of fitting her out for her new duties was carried out in Douglas by the Steam Packet Company's own workshops.

She worked strenuously and successfully on service, mainly without much incident, and she carried British and American troops on the two-way traffic to and from France.

On February 6, 1917, she left Southampton on a fine night with a full moon, with more than a thousand troops on board. Less than an hour's steaming from Le Havre a German U-boat surfaced almost dead ahead and not more than 200 yards away. The troopship kept on course and when within ten yards of the submarine Captain Cain of the *Mona's Queen* saw a torpedo travel underneath his ship and track away to starboard. The U-boat was almost instantaneously hit by the port paddlebox of the *Mona's Queen* and sank at once. The steel paddle floats of the wheel had rammed home into the enemy's conning tower.

The collision damaged the vessel, which managed to steam slowly to Le Havre. The troops were disembarked. The *Mona's Queen* set off under tow for major repair work in Southampton. The weather was bad and the Captain decided to complete the journey without aid while the tug stood by. She eventually reached Southampton in more than twice her normal time.

After repairs she returned to trooping in March, 1917. Three years later she was back on station in the Steam Packet fleet, the last of its paddlers.

* * *

The *King Orry* (III) was fitted out as a boarding vessel by Cammell Laird's in late November, 1914, and left for Scapa Flow. There she spent her time on patrol, tending to the crews of stricken ships, challenging suspects, and putting prize crews aboard where appropriate. On one occasion she sent men aboard a large vessel laden with 10,000 tons of wheat for Germany, and her prize crew took the vessel into Kirkwall. Then, diverted to patrol down the fringe of the German minefield off Heligoland, she challenged and boarded six ships in one day, and put a prize crew aboard an oil tanker which she then directed to the East Coast.

After the Battle of Jutland the Royal Navy was ordered intensive gunnery practice and the *King Orry* turned to the business of target towing. She was well suited to this work and was able to move the largest target at more than 12 knots. She even accompanied the Grand Fleet on exercises and acted as a "repeating ship", that is, she transmitted the flagship signals to the battle squadron in line astern. Later she was used for training gunners. In all, a busy life.

In 1916 the *King Orry* was disguised as a peaceful trader, substantially changed in appearance, and sent to patrol off Norway under the name of *Viking Orry*. There she was to intercept ships carrying contraband to Germany down the Scandinavian approach. Through fair weather and foul, but more usually foul in those northern waters, the *King Orry* stayed at the job, suffering much storm damage and at one time was ordered down to Liverpool for repairs. She reached what had once been her regular port of call, but not before a shore battery at New Brighton had put shots across her bow when she failed to give a satisfactory answer to questioning signals.

She continued this industrious record for the rest of the War. When the German Fleet surrendered at Scapa Flow on November 21, 1918, she was the sole representative of the British mercantile marine at the capitulation ceremony. Admiral Beatty awarded her the place of honour in the middle of the centre line. So a small Manx steamer took station, surrounded by the victorious British Grand Fleet. It was symbolic of the work and sacrifice of the small ships.

The *King Orry* went back to the Steam Packet Company, and after some 20 years service she went to war again.

King Orry leads the German Fleet to Scapa Flow, 1918   MANX MUSEUM

The *Queen Victoria* and the *Prince of Wales* were fitted out as net-laying anti-submarine craft. They had been sold to the Admiralty in 1915 and never returned to the Steam Packet Company's fleet.

They were paddle-steamers and they were getting on in years — they had been built in 1888 — but were still reasonably fast for their day; naval architects appeared to think that paddlers, if not converted as troop carriers, were well suited to this anti-submarine work.

The two ships were soon in the Eastern Mediterranean theatre, in support of troopships and even warships in submarine-infested seas.

At one time during the Gallipoli fighting they found themselves accompanying their own *Snaefell*, which was landing troops at Suvla Bay.

Prince of Wales (renamed *Prince Edward*) on active service   IMPERIAL WAR MUSEUM

Tynwald (III) (below) and *Fenella*(I) (facing page) maintained the Douglas-Liverpool
service throughout the four years of the war

The *Tynwald* (III) shared the Douglas-Liverpool run with the *Fenella* through the 1914/18 War. She had a number of close encounters with floating mines but was never hit; the mine-sweepers worked day and night to keep the approaches to Liverpool open, and although there were casualties they were relatively few.

On April 9, 1917, a German submarine had penetrated to within a few miles of Liverpool and succeeded in torpedoing the American liner *New York*. The *Tynwald* was inward bound from Douglas and was quickly on the scene. There were 600 passengers aboard the liner, including Admiral Sims of the U.S. Navy. The *Tynwald* took them safely on board and landed them at Liverpool. The *New York* was taken in tow by tugs and eventually docked.

Manxman converted to an aircraft carrier   IMPERIAL WAR MUSEUM

The wartime record of the *Manxman* must be mentioned, although she was not a Company ship until purchased in 1920. She was owned by the old Midland Railway when commissioned in December, 1916, at Chatham, after she had been converted to a seaplane carrier.

She served in support of the Grand Fleet until October, 1917, and was then transferred to the Eastern Mediterranean. She lacked the speed of the *Ben-my-Chree* and the *Viking* and she had lost her place in the entourage of the Grand Fleet because her conversion had made her just too slow. The C.-in-C. of the Fleet, Admiral Sir David Beatty, wrote a letter from HMS *Iron Duke* on January 11, 1917, in which he said that the *Manxman* was unfit for service with the Battle Cruiser Fleet "owing to her lack of speed." These last six words had been added in his own handwriting.

However, she had made one contribution to naval aviation history. She had introduced the Sopwith Pup single-seater fighter. It could take off from her launching platform in only 20 feet in a 20 knot wind.

The mathematics were in the fighter's favour; its wing loading was only five pounds per square foot and its power loading 16.4 pounds per horsepower.

The small machine had a Le Rhone engine of 80 h.p., giving it a speed of 112 m.p.h. at sea level and 103 m.p.h. at 9,000 feet. It had a ceiling of 17,500 feet and a fuel endurance of three hours. Flotation bags were used to enable it to land alongside the *Manxman* and it was then hoisted aboard.

At the war's end she arrived at Plymouth on the same day as the *Viking*, then HMS *Vindex*. She paid off in May, 1919, and joined the Steam Packet Company the following year.

The war was over. The Manx fleet was back on station.

CHAPTER SIX: *The Years Between*

WITH THE END OF THE FIRST WORLD WAR
a spasmodic and uneasy peace settled on Europe for 21 disturbed years. It was a time of
international suspicion and tension culminating in the rise of the dictators and the wars and
invasions that lead remorselessly to the next holocaust. Yet within a year of Armistice Day,
1918, the holidaymakers were returning to the Isle of Man and before long it seemed to the
islanders to be a matter of business as usual.

The switch from war to peace meant a dramatic turnaround in the Steam Packet
Company's business. In 1914 it had carried 404,481 passengers to the Island, the great majority
of them holidaymakers. From 1915 to 1918 the figures dropped dramatically. The official
statistics give 33,768 as the incoming figure for 1915; 52,600 for 1916; 50,858 for 1917, and
96,593 for 1918.

This work was carried out by the Company's four smallest vessels; they also brought food
and other vital supplies not only for the resident population, but for the Service personnel and
the 28,000 internees who were confined in Knockaloe and other centres on the island.

With the end of the war the Company found itself liberally endowed with cash earned by
the charter or sale of many of its ships to the Admiralty, but it was in urgent need of new
tonnage to handle the expected peacetime traffic. However, industry as a whole was in a
disorganised and seriously rundown state after the exhaustion of the fighting and vast
munition effort, and vessels could not possibly be built in time for the tourist influx of 1919 and
1920. The Company compromised by buying the *Mona* (IV) in 1919, and the *Manxman* (I),
Mona's Isle (IV) and *Snaefell* (IV) the following year.

These four second-hand vessels augmented the seven ships that remained of the
Company's pre-war fleet. The small cargo boat *Tyrconnel* and the *Douglas* (III), *Tynwald* (III),
and *Fenella* (I) had maintained the island lifeline during the war. Not one of the four had a
tonnage of 1,000 tons. Apart from this quartet the Admiralty had returned the *Mona's Queen*
(II), the *King Orry* (III) and the *Peel Castle* to the Company. It was vital to increase the
passenger-carrying capacity of the fleet, and for the summer season of 1919 the Steam Packet
chartered *La Marguerite*, a paddle steamer that could carry some 1,500 passengers, from the
Liverpool & North Wales S.S. Co. Ltd. after her return from troop carrying.

All these vessels only gave the Company a total carrying capacity of less than 10,000 in its
first season after the war, whereas the pre-war figure had been in excess of 20,000. Yet in
1919, as had been expected, the return of the holidaymakers really started; the incoming
passenger traffic totalled 343,332. It was substantially down on the pre-war years and very
much below the figures of the first decade of the century. However, aircraft and continental
package holidays were still no real threat, and the figures mounted to a plateau of around
550,000 in the 1930's. Despite the political tensions in Europe it seemed at least a case of full
steam ahead in the Isle of Man. The strain on the Steam Packet Company was severe.

La Marguerite disembarks passengers at Victoria Pier in 1919.

The records show the following figures of incoming passengers from 1920 onwards.

1920	561,124	1930	487,404
1921	427,923	1931	451,078
1922	481,736	1932	478,947
1923	447,826	1933	502,329
1924	446,834	1934	533,912
1925	540,628	1935	536,699
1926	384,705	1936	552,981
1927	526,881	1937	583,037
1928	550,572	1938	535,969
1929	555,211	1939	552,457

These arrivals were almost wholly from the Company steamers. Aircraft passengers were not included and when they did start they accounted for hundreds rather than thousands over the entire season. In graph form the returns show a wavering line, a high point in 1920, when the United Kingdom seemed to be settling down to some sort of normality, and a heavy drop in 1926 when British society was challenged by a General Strike and a very protracted coal strike that seriously damaged the whole of industry.

Although these at first glance seem to be healthy tourist figures over the years the Company, like the rest of Britain, was experiencing great difficulties. These were times of profound change; resettlement after 1918 proved a slow and painful business. A Board meeting in Douglas at the end of 1924 revealed that there had been a small increase in the number of passengers carried during the season, but the cash income was down by a few thousand pounds owing to "a still further transfer from saloon to steerage bookings due to the continued industrial depression on the mainland". Meanwhile it had been deemed wise to reduce freight rates and working expenses had been cut; on the other hand, the cost of overhauls had increased. It was a typical picture of near-slump industrial conditions.

Two years later the major strikes of 1926 seriously disrupted passenger schedules. The bunkers emptied; dock gates closed; freight stood still. Ships had to be laid up. The *Fenella*, *Tyrconnel* and the *Cushag* were taken out of service and foodstuffs were imported into the Island by the passenger boats. Plans for a number of charter sailings had to be abandoned. The route between Douglas and Liverpool was maintained by the *Manxman* (I) and the *Manx Maid* (I), which were oil fuelled. On May 20, 1926, the Steam Packet Board was obliged to order that sailings between these ports should be reduced to a single passage each way daily, with one extra service on Saturday and Monday afternoons.

Yet while these industrial and labour troubles continued intermittently for years the Steam Packet directors still found time for charitable matters. Men worked to an advanced age in those days, and planned pension schemes were almost unknown. Yet when a Superintendent Engineer retired at the age of 76 he was granted a pension of £500 a year although his salary had been only £800. The gesture was extremely generous for its day. Even as the Company was recovering from the strikes of the mid-1920's the Trustees of King William's College, in the Isle of Man, issued a public appeal for £50,000 towards its centenary fund. The Steam Packet directors resolved that as the Company had derived considerable revenue from the College and its boys it should contribute £500.

The school and the shipping company had, in fact, had a close relationship for many years. Hundreds of the lads used its steamers every year. At the end of each vacation they would storm off the steamer at Douglas and rush along the North Quay to the station to catch the special train that took them to the school at Castletown. Their favourite sport on this journey was to jump from the carriages during the slow climb up the steep gradient to Port Soderick, trot along the line and jump aboard once more as the engine gathered speed again.

Pension and donation . . . . . In such ways did the Company help in years of hardship.

King Orry (III) went aground at New Brighton in August 1921.

The *Ben-my-Chree* (IV) was the first of five ships the Company ordered to be built between the two wars. The Cammell Laird yards were beset with serious problems in the aftermath of the crippling General Strike of May 1926, and the protracted coal strike that went on for months in the same year. However, the builders met their deadline despite many anxieties, the ship was launched on April 5, 1927, and a very considerable success she was throughout her working life of 38 years. She represented a high standard of interior decoration and furnishing, virtues that had been a feature of Steam Packet vessels since the earliest days of the Company. The cost of such fittings today would be prohibitive, quite apart from the fact that they would not be allowed by international regulations. The main first-class passenger staircase of the *Ben*, for instance, was made of walnut, and splendid it undoubtedly looked.

Launch of the *Ben-my-Chree* (IV) at Birkenhead

STEWART BALE

First class Lounge (above) and

STEWART BALE

Sleeping Lounge on *Ben-my-Chree* (IV).

First class Smoke Room (above) and

STEWART BALE

Tea Room on *Ben-my-Chree* (IV).

Special State Room on *Ben-my-Chree* (IV)   STEWART BALE

The inter-war years saw the decorative side of ship architecture at its most ambitious. Rich woodwork, expensive drapes and thick carpeting gave elegance to many a passenger ship. The fashion started to change as the Second World War approached. New and colourful building materials were being introduced. The Western world was moving steadily into the age of synthetics. Much more urgently, of course, newer and even more stringent safety regulations for ships were being introduced internationally. The Americans especially had an unwelcome number of marine fires, of which the disaster to the *Morro Castle* in the years leading up to the Second World War was the worst. This made them extra cautious and their policy was one of less and less woodwork and more and more steel. One retired sea captain put it simply: "New regulations were coming out all the time." Preventative measures insisted on by one country had to be tested and if deemed sound had to be adopted by others. In this way the fire and safety precautions multiplied and by the late 50's and 60's the elaborate elegance of old had gone for good. The baroque had given way to the streamlined.

Peveril (II) launched at Birkenhead in 1929　　　　　　　　　　　　STEWART BALE

A year after the *Ben-my-Chree* went into service the Steam Packet bought in three more secondhand ships — the *Victoria, Ramsey Town* and *Rushen Castle* — all three having been originally built for United Kingdom railway companies. And after another year the Company ordered the building of the *Peveril* (II), the first modern cargo ship built directly for it.

This was a prelude to the important event of 1930 — the building by Vickers Armstrong of the Company's centenary ship, the *Lady of Mann* (I), which at 3,104 tons was the largest steamer to be built for the line. Once again the new vessel reflected the highest standard of fitment and decoration, of a lavishness impossible after the Second World War. The polished wood finishes of the 1930's were by then becoming things of the past.

The order for the vessel had been placed with Vickers Armstrong on July 3, 1929. The times were pinched and work proceeded smoothly. There were none of the complications that had bedevilled the building of the *Ben-my-Chree* (IV). The keel was laid on October 19 and the plating was completed on January 27, 1930. She was launched on March 4 and in service by the end of June.

One of the most elegant features of the centenary *Lady of Mann* was its main staircase made of mahogany. It was widely admired, and was another example of the type of furnishing that had to vanish. Before the ship had finished her service the staircase was in contravention of the fire regulations. Alterations had to be made in the mid-sixties: the stylish opening had to be blocked in with steel walls and steel doors fitted. The appearance was largely sacrificed; the regulations concerning fire precautions duly satisfied. But when the *Lady* was due to be broken up in the early 1970's the fine staircase was not quite finished. An enthusiast living in Castletown succeeded in acquiring at least part of the woodwork and reassembled it in a private house.

The Centenary ship, *Lady of Mann* (I), launched at Barrow in 1930.

Her main First Class staircase which was made of mahogany.

Tea Room (above) Private Cabin (facing page)

STEWART BALE

and Sleeping Accommodation on *Lady of Mann* (I).

Mona's Queen (III) was painted white and green for her launching at Birkenhead in 1934.   STEWART BALE

Ben-my-Chree (IV)

Lady of Mann (I)

and Mona's Queen (III)

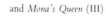

all shared the attractive white over green colour scheme in the thirties.

From 1931 onwards the North Wales steamer, *St. Seiriol* (II) was a regular visitor to Douglas harbour bringing thousands of day trippers from Llandudno.

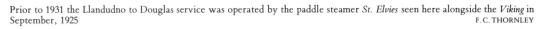

Prior to 1931 the Llandudno to Douglas service was operated by the paddle steamer *St. Elvies* seen here alongside the *Viking* in September, 1925

F. C. THORNLEY

Four years later, in 1934, the *Mona's Queen* (III) was launched. She was the leader of the last three ships, all twin-screw, geared turbines, to be built for the Company before the Second World War. The *Fenella* (II) and the *Tynwald* (IV) followed her into service in 1937. It was the grim misfortune of war that not one of the three survived into the uneasy peace.

In October, 1936, came a development that was a precursor of more important installations ahead. The Isle of Man Harbour Board installed a Wireless Directional Beacon, known as the Marconi TW3, on the Victoria Pier. The instrument used a medium wavelength, enabling the ordinary receiver of the type usually carried by ships to pick up its signal and thus plot a guide line to the Pier, especially valuable in fog. The Steam Packet Company took a decision promptly; they proposed to instal the necessary receivers on all their vessels.

Negotiations began with the Marconi Company. By January, 1937, agreement had been reached. A directional Wireless Apparatus, as the instrument was called, was to be installed on every ship; the fee would be £7 per month per set, with a minimum of four months, which could cover most of the purely seasonal sailings. For longer periods the charge would not exceed £40 in a year, less 5 per cent commission.

The Board estimated that the total hire cost would be about £486 a year for the whole fleet. They were well satisfied.

International affairs took an ominous turn in 1936 with the remilitarization of the Rhineland by the Nazis and soon tension was rising throughout Europe. The effect on the industrial scene in Great Britain was complex. Precautionary moves were being taken step by step. In September 1938, around the time of the Munich crisis, the Board considered a letter from the Director of Sea Transport giving the Company formal notice that the *Manx Maid* and the *King Orry* were required for urgent Government service and were thus requisitioned. However, the tension eased and another letter a week later indicated that the matter was suspended. The word "suspended" was certainly apt. Five months later, in February 1939, following letters from the Shipping Federation and the Board of Trade, Steam Packet crews were being trained in air raid precaution duties. They attended instruction classes given by members of the Douglas Police Force.

Events were now moving as a ship on the slipway. In April, 1939, the Company directors were attempting to go about their normal business and were discussing a proposed new head office building at Douglas; a month later they found themselves obliged to agree that owing to the extreme shortage of pilots they must accept a drastic restriction of the schedules of Isle of Man Air Services, in which they had an important interest. Then in a few weeks the Mercantile Marine Department of the Board of Trade wrote to say that six Steam Packet vessels were under consideration for use as troop transports in the event of a major war emergency.

Whatever may have been said of the politicians it could not be denied that the Service departments were thinking ahead, ready to deploy scant resources.

CHAPTER SEVEN: *At War Again*

Tʜᴇ ꜰɪʀꜱᴛ ᴡᴏʀʟᴅ ᴡᴀʀ ʜᴀᴅ ꜱᴛᴀʀᴛᴇᴅ ᴏɴ ᴀ quiet note in the Isle of Man. Belgium had seemed so far away. The Second brought the island an immediate and special involvement. Much precautionary preparation had been carried out and on the declaration the official machine was at work.

Almost at once orders were given to a number of hotel owners, boarding-house keepers, and even householders, that they must vacate their premises in a week and leave them empty. Room had to be found to house detainees who would be collected from the mainland for internment. These people were not enemies; they were not prisoners. They were a special category. And they were destined for the Isle of Man.

The average Manxman did not fully know who was coming to fill these vacant houses. Such matters were secret. All the islanders really knew was that on parts of the front at Douglas the pneumatic drills were soon busy. Stanchions were going into position along the promenade. The barbed wire was on its way.

Before all this began the Steam Packet Company had had orders. Away in distant Whitehall the Admiralty had planned ahead. A substantial part of Britain's large merchant fleet was requisitioned even before war started.

The Company's ships were involved. The *King Orry*, the *Mona's Isle*, and the *Manx Maid* had been called up a week earlier. The *Mona's Queen* was under orders on September 2, 1939, the last day of ominous peace. The *Viking*, *Tynwald*, *Fenella* and *Manxman* were all commandeered within a few days of the outbreak. The *Lady of Mann* and the *Ben-my-Chree* followed later that same week.

At the declaration the Steam Packet Company had a fleet of 16 ships. Its ten best vessels went into various forms of active service, four to be lost. The *Rushen Castle* and the *Snaefell* were kept on to maintain the vital link with the mainland, the latter as a relief vessel. For a time the *Victoria* joined them. The *Peveril*, *Conister* and *Cushag* were of smaller tonnage and they stayed on to handle freight. The *Cushag* was sold for scrap in 1943.

However. the Company's first participation in the War came not from the ships that were being hurried through the fitting-out process to prepare them for active service, but from the relatively humble *Rushen Castle* and the *Victoria*.

These were the vessels that brought the first of the detainees to the island. They came over in batches under guard, segregated from the civilian passengers. The first arrivals were only a very small fraction of the number who were later to be held as the war developed.

The *King Orry* (III), veteran of World War I, was one of three Company ships to be fitted out as an armed boarding vessel — an ABV — in the Second. This meant that she became a Royal Navy vessel in the full sense, flying the White Ensign and being officered and manned by naval crew, four of whom were Steam Packet men who had joined the Royal Navy for war duty. The other IOMSP ships that served in the war were classed as personnel vessels, mainly

King Orry (III)
veteran of World War I,
was sunk at Dunkirk in
May 1940.

used for troop carrying and similar operations. They were unarmed. They came under the Ministry of War Transport and remained as merchant navy units, flying the Red Ensign and crewed by Company personnel.

On September 27, 1939, the *King Orry* was commissioned and assigned to the Dover Command. She served as an ABV from Dover until May 22, 1940, when she was taken off her normal duties to stand by for the likely evacuation from Dunkirk. She then became one of the armada of small ships that helped to make possible the grimmest and yet most successful evacuation ever undertaken by an army in the West.

Operation Dynamo had been planned under increasingly critical conditions, with Admiral Ramsay in command at Dover. The first troops were brought off the Dunkirk beaches on the night of May 26, after the signal to start the evacuation had been given a few minutes before seven that spring evening. In all nearly 900 ships took part in the desperate work of the next ten days, nearly 250 of them being lost.

Among them was the *King Orry*. She started and finished, early. The scene at Dunkirk can be imagined. The almost continual air attacks and the fire from the heavy German armour made survival seem impossible for both men and ships. The wrecks and casualties mounted as the rescuing vessels pressed forward into a relentless bombardment. To the men of the merchant fleets it must have been almost, but not quite, unendurable.

The *King Orry* carried some armament as an ABV. She was under the command of Cdr. J. Elliott, RNR, and he succeeded in getting into the harbour and embarking 1,131 soldiers. The ship cast off and made for Dover in the early hours of May 27. Shore batteries off Calais opened up on her shortly after nine in the morning. She was damaged and there were casualties aboard. However, she was able to continue to Dover, where she docked before noon.

The ship returned to Dunkirk in the late afternoon of May 29. She survived a dive bombing attack and made for the East Pier. A second and heavier attack was made on her; her steering gear was put out of action and all bridge instruments and woodwork were shattered. Even, then, after colliding with the pier, the *King Orry* was still able to secure alongside.

More air attacks followed: when darkness came it was possible to see where she had been holed and to make temporary repairs. But in this condition she was a danger to shipping that was already in enough danger. She might founder in the approach channel to the harbour. However, after midnight the ship was ordered to leave and her commander succeeded in getting the badly damaged vessel clear of the harbour entrance.

Soon she began to list badly to starboard. Her engine room started to flood and she was abandoned. Shortly after two in the morning of May 30, 1940, she sank. Other ships in the crowded and turbulent waters closed in and survivors, including the four Manx engineers, were picked up.

Mona's Isle (IV) also served in both World Wars.   MANX MUSEUM

The *Mona's Isle* (IV) was also a veteran, 34 years old, when the Second World War broke out. She had seen service in the 1914-18 War as the *Onward* in the colours of the South Eastern and Chatham Railway. Her record as an ABV for the first months of war until Dunkirk was largely uneventful. Her record from May 22, 1940, was anything but.

According to Ministry of Defence records the *Mona's Isle* was the first ship to leave Dover for Dunkirk when Operation Dynamo started, except for HMS *Wolsey*, a destroyer which was to act as a radio link ship. She berthed in Dunkirk harbour during an air attack and took off 1,420 troops. The *Mona's Isle* was then fired on by shore batteries as she steamed past Gravelines early the following morning. Little more than 20 minutes later she was heavily machine gunned from the air. The result was 83 casualties, including 23 killed. She reached Dover safely however, escorted by a destroyer, HMS *Windsor*. The mission had taken nearly 15 hours and she was recorded as the first ship to complete the round trip during the evacuation.

Two awards were later made to members of the ship's company for their part in the action that night. The Commanding Officer, Crd. J. C. K. Dowding, RNR, received the Distinguished Service Order. Petty Officer L. B. Kearley-Pope, RNR, was awarded the Distinguished Service Medal. He had remained at a 12-pounder gun despite multiple wounds and he took a great risk in coming out of cover to close cordite boxes. There were casualties among the gun's crew, but the PO continued to carry out his duties until the ship berthed six hours later. He was in hospital for nearly six weeks, but returned to active service and survived the war.

Cdr. Dowding was later promoted to Captain. He was Commodore of the ill-fated convoy PQ 17 to Russia, which was forced to scatter and suffered heavy losses in July, 1942.

The *Mona's Isle* made a second round trip to Dunkirk, bringing out a further 1,200 troops, and bringing her total to 2,634. The rest of her war service was spent either as an ABV or an accommodation ship. Before she was transferred to the Tyne in 1941 she was three times involved in collisions, one of which did extensive damage and sent her to dock for three months. Once on the Tyne, where she lent support to the AA defences of coastal convoys, she gave valuable assistance on two occasions to merchantmen that had been bombed, in one case rescuing 32 survivors. After D-Day she worked on cross-Channel transport duties until June, 1945, was then chartered by the Ministry of War Transport and finally released in March, 1946.

* * *

The *Manx Maid* (I) had seen service in World War I under her original name, *Caesarea*. In World War II she was requisitioned on August 27, 1939, as an ABV. She took no part in the Dunkirk evacuation as she had been undergoing repairs at the time. She was then ordered to Southampton and she made two crossings into the war zone as the retreat moved west along the French coast. Her first mission took her to St. Malo, but it was already occupied by the Germans. She escaped after being unable to go inshore, and returned to England. She then went to Brest and in her one trip brought out nearly 3,000 troops, roughly twice her allowable passenger complement. She pulled away in a heavy swell followed by the *Lady of Mann* and a British cross-Channel railway steamer. The acting Master, long since in retirement, recalls how the vessel was almost two feet below her marks so that she developed condenser trouble and had to heave to for nearly three hours some distance off the French coast with the main enemy force about 30 miles from the port. Even so, she reached Plymouth safely.

She was later renamed the *Bruce* by the Royal Navy and from the end of 1942 she became a Fleet Air Arm Target vessel, continuing those duties until March, 1945.

She was paid off at Ardrossan on March 21, 1945, and returned to the Steam Packet Company that day.

* * *

The *Mona's Queen* had been requisitioned as a personnel vessel on the day the war broke out. As such she remained a merchantman with a Steam Packet Captain and crew. She spent most of May, 1940 taking off refugees from Dutch and French ports as the massive German advance swept forward to the Channel. On May 22 she left Boulogne for Dover with 2,000 British troops aboard.

Her record during the Dunkirk evacuation was short. She started under Captain R. Duggan and arrived back in Dover during the night of May 27 with 1,200 troops. She was shelled by shore guns off the French coast the next day but she escaped damage. On May 29 the troops on the Dunkirk beaches were short of drinking water, so the *Mona's Queen* loaded water canisters and sailed from Dover in the early morning. She hit a mine a mile off Dunkirk harbour at 5.30 a.m. and sank in two minutes. Captain A. Holkham, who had taken over as Master, and 31 members of the crew, were picked up by destroyers. Twenty-four of the crew were lost. All but ten of them had worked in the engine room. They included the Chief and Second Engineer. Seventeen of the dead were from the Isle of Man.

Mona's Queen (III) mined and lost off Dunkirk.   IMPERIAL WAR MUSEUM

The *Viking*, another veteran of the First World War, in which she had done important service as an early aircraft carrier, was requisitioned in the first week of the Second World War as a personnel vessel. She then acted as a transport, mainly to Cherbourg from Southampton.

The *Viking* did not take part in the critical Dunkirk operation, for she had recently been bombed when in the Thames Estuary and was undergoing repairs. But she was very active in the later stages of the withdrawal from France.

Captained by James Bridson with Edward Gelling and Harry Kinley as Chief and Second Officers, she was present at the evacuation from Le Havre, and later from Cherbourg. She also had an unusual mission in the Channel Islands. She steamed into St. Peter Port, Guernsey, prepared to take off evacuees. Her master was offered 1,800 schoolchildren, representing virtually the entire juvenile population of the island. He took them aboard and landed them at Weymouth, steaming undamaged through occasional air raids on the way.

At the end of that phase of the war in northern France she proceeded to Barrow and then for a short time returned to the Isle of Man and resumed her civilian run between Fleetwood and Douglas. She was requisitioned again, and served as a Fleet Air Arm target vessel based on Crail for seven months from June, 1942. From December 1943 until 1945 she was a personnel ship; during much of this time she worked on the cross-Channel transport service. She missed the D-Day invasion having been hit by a flying bomb while being serviced in the Surrey Commercial Docks in London. The fact that she was a coal burner made her a difficult ship to fit into the modern pattern; she needed frequent bunkering and this was inconvenient in major fleet movements.

She was taken out of war support service in June, 1945, and subsequently returned to her owners.

Another veteran of the First World War, *Viking* is seen here in November, 1942.   ROYAL NAVY

Steam Packet losses in the Second World War included their three newest vessels. *Tynwald* (IV) seen here during the war was lost off North Africa in 1942.   IMPERIAL WAR MUSEUM

IL-I

The *Tynwald* (IV) had the distinction of embarking more troops at Dunkirk than any other Steam Packet Company ship. Hers was a fine record. She was requisitioned as a personnel vessel in the first week of the war and her log was largely uneventful until Operation Dynamo started. At the time her Master was Captain J. H. Whiteway, followed by Captain W. A. Qualtrough.

She made her first mission to Dunkirk on May 28 and was one of ten personnel vessels that lifted a total of 14,760 troops from the East Pier on the following day. In the late evening of May 30 she was one of the four personnel vessels back at the pier, and her own lift was 1,153 troops. On June 2 she made her third trip and embarked 1,200 troops, leaving for Dover in the early morning of June 3.

The last day of the operation was June 4; shortly after 2.0 in the afternoon the Admiralty announced that Operation Dynamo was closed down.

By then the *Tynwald* had already left the East Pier after her fourth trip. She was the last ship and she landed 3,000 French troops in England later that day.

Her total in the operation was officially given as 8,953 troops.

At the end of 1940 she was compulsorily acquired, fitted out as an auxiliary anti-aircraft ship and commissioned as HMS *Tynwald* on October 1, 1941. After a year on convoy escort duties around Britain she was assigned to Operation Torch, the Allied landing in North Africa, and was involved in the attack on Algiers on November 8, 1942.

Three days later the ship was part of a task force sent to capture an airfield near Bougie, 100 miles east of Algiers. At the centre of the force were infantry landing craft, and the cover included the cruiser *Sheffield*, a monitor, HMS *Roberts*, the *Tynwald*, and fourteen supporting vessels.

The first landing met with no opposition and the Bougie harbour was occupied; but it proved impossible to capture the airfield from the sea owing to adverse weather conditions. Instead, the attacking force that was still at sea came under heavy air attack.

On November 12 the *Tynwald* was hit either by a mine or a torpedo. She had been standing by the monitor *Roberts*, which was on fire and badly damaged.

The *Tynwald* went down in seven fathoms of water. Three officers and seven ratings were listed as casualties.

*   *   *

The *Fenella* (II) had the shortest war history of all the Steam Packet Company vessels. In the first week of the War she had been requisitioned as a personnel carrier.

Her first few months were uneventful. Then, on May 28, 1940, she went to Dunkirk, her first trip into the evacuation area. Her Master was Captain W. Cubbon. She started to embark troops from the East Pier, and had 650 on board when she came under heavy fire in the third massed air attack of that day. She was hit by three bombs in quick succession. The first attack struck her promenade deck, the second hit the pier, blowing lumps of concrete through the ship's side below the waterline, and the third exploded between the pier and the ship's side, wrecking the engine room.

The *Fenella* was abandoned and later sank. The troops were disembarked on to the pier, where they were picked up by the famous old London pleasure steamer, the *Crested Eagle*. This too, was subsequently bombed and beached.

The survivors of the *Fenella*'s crew were later picked up by a Dutch skoot, the *Patria*, which was under Royal Navy command. Others of the crew had succeeded in getting ashore on to the pier and had then been taken on to the *Crested Eagle*, only to receive a direct hit.

The *Fenella* had gone into the harbour with a crew of 48, all Steam Packet men and most of them Manxmen. Four men had been left behind on leave. In all, 33 men succeeded in getting back to Dover, where one died of wounds. Many had been wounded, some seriously.

Some weeks later a postcard was received from a Liverpool lad, T. Helsby, a 19-year-old junior steward. He had last been seen, terribly burned, as the ship was foundering after the bomb attack. It transpired that he had been taken prisoner of war — the only Steam Packet Company man to be taken prisoner in all the operations of its ships in wartime — and was in a hospital in Belgium. The German surgeons did an expert job on him and he was repatriated before the end of the war. He returned later to the Steam Packet Company and is now chief steward of the *Ben-my-Chree*.

The sinking of the *Fenella* was later followed by a theory that the ship had been raised by the enemy, fitted with new engines, and used under the name *Reval*. Much later the belief grew that she had then been taken over by the Russians, following the collapse of Germany.

F. B. O'Friel has arrived at what is probably the authentic version after help from a correspondent who searched the German naval files at Frieburg. From the papers unearthed it seems certain that the wrecked *Fenella* was eventually removed piecemeal from the harbour as scrap. The Germans had classified her as Wreck No. 11. Near her had been Wreck No. 8, the steamer *Bawtry*. This ship was raised in March 1941, was later repaired in Antwerp and then declared a prize of war. She was taken over by a Kiel shipping firm in 1943 under the name of *Rival*, only to be completely destroyed in the massive R.A.F. air raid on Hamburg on the night of December 31, 1944.

*   *   *

The *Manxman* had started the First World War in the colours of the Midland Railway Company, and had been converted to an aircraft carrier. In the Second World War she was requisitioned by the Ministry of War Transport as a personnel vessel.

She served at the Dunkirk evacuation in 1940. On May 29 she was one of ten personnel ships which together took off 14,760 troops from the East Pier. She returned to Dunkirk on the morning of June 2, when the operation was getting near its close, and embarked 177 troops. In all she took off 2,394 men.

No sooner had the *Manxman* returned from her final journey to Dunkirk than she was ordered west to Dartmouth, where she had the ironical experience of being fired on by a small guard boat that obviously had not been alerted to her arrival.

Within a few hours she was redirected to Southampton. This was the start of her most active phase in the entire war. The evacuation of the ports of north-west France was beginning and the *Manxman* knew the coast well, having spent some months before Dunkirk carrying troops to Le Havre and Cherbourg.

Within what seemed a few days she made a succession of trips to the French ports under the Command of Captain P. B. Cowley. At Cherbourg she embarked retreating Allied troops as the enemy approached the port, and returned to Southampton, often under air attack. Once back on the South Coast of England she disembarked the men she had brought back, refuelled, and was off again almost at once. It was dangerous and sleepless work well remebered by veterans from the *Manxman*'s officers and crew, among whom were Chief Officer Lyndhurst Callow, and Second Officer A. W. G. Kissack, who later became the Company's Marine Superintendent. As the days advanced the shelling came nearer, the raids more frequent, and the Cherbourg harbour area necessarily more congested with survival boats, wrecks, and the debris of battle. It was Dunkirk again, but on a smaller scale. Meanwhile the *Manxman*, with no protective armament of her own, went in and out of the firing.

As conditions became desperate and further Allied evacuation became impossible the destroyer L.11. was specially sent at full speed of 36 knots from Portsmouth to help cover the *Manxman*'s escape. Chief Officer Callow, who survived to become Commodore of the Steam Packet Company fleet, vividly recalls how the ship eventually pulled out from Cherbourg. The large cranes along the dockside had been blasted and broken, and were one of the many hazards to shipping. Tanks were approaching the harbour area; the remnants of the Allied armies were fighting them off as best they could. The *Manxman* herself was laden with troops and with stacked ammunition, small arms and even field weapons saved from the catastrophe. One hit from a bombing aircraft could have blown up the entire ship. Despite the odds, she escaped. Her crew had been forced to cut her mooring ropes with axes. There was no longer any harbour staff. The *Manxman* then pulled out, thanks to the fire cover given them by the Royal Navy destroyer, which turned her forward guns on to the German tank column as it advanced down the quayside.

Rommel is even said to have referred to the *Manxman* in his papers, describing her as a "cheeky two-funnel steamer". When she pulled out for the last time his main army was only a few miles away. The net was closing fast.

The *Manxman*'s main duties were at Cherbourg, but she was also deeply involved at the small port of St. Malo, to the east, where she was the last ship out of harbour.

In October, 1941, she was fitted out as an RDF (Radio Direction Finding) vessel, and taken over by the Admiralty and commissioned as HMS *Caduceus*. She was then ordered to Douglas, her home port in peacetime, on the cliff above which there was one of the early radar training stations. From Douglas she spent some time on patrol in the Irish Sea, while naval personnel were initiated into the new mysteries of precision radio direction finding.

Manxman escaped from Cherbourg with the help of a destroyer.

Mishaps resulted. The *Manxman* was twice damaged when colliding with the Victoria Pier, Douglas, and was sent to Belfast for repairs.

Thence she went to the Clyde and continued her radar training duties, only to be driven ashore near Greenock in a fierce gale in February 1943. She was reconditioned and returned to personnel vessel duties. She acted as a troop carrier and eventually moved to the traffic between Harwich and Tilbury and the Belgian and Dutch ports, bringing over service personnel, civilians and displaced persons. The war over, she was a tired ship, and was eventually sold for scrap in 1949.

Lady of Mann (I) evacuated troops from Dunkirk, Le Havre, Cherbourg and Brest.

The *Lady of Mann* had a very eventful record during the war; she served at Dunkirk under Captain T. C. Woods and then at the evacuation of the north-western French ports. After this she spent four years on transport work from Lerwick. She then went south and was engaged in the D-Day landings on the Cherbourg peninsula.

Her Dunkirk record was spectacular. Requisitioned as a personnel ship at the outbreak of war, she had a good turn of speed and was able to get in and out of the Dunkirk bombardments and lift 4,262 men back to the relative safety of Dover and Folkestone. She remained for six hours in Dunkirk harbour on May 31, 1940, despite having been damaged by shellfire from shore batteries on her approach and being bombed by enemy aircraft. She emerged from the bombing with little damage and claimed one aircraft shot down. She was back at Dunkirk in the early hours of June 1 and took off 1,500 casualties.

The following day, June 2, she again steamed into Dunkirk but was ordered back for lack of troops. The evacuation was drawing towards its close. She picked up 18 French soldiers from a small boat on the way back and landed them in England. On the night of June 3 she made her last trip to the shattered harbour. She berthed alongside the East Pier at a little after midnight on the morning of June 4, and left for England after embarking another 1,244 troops in little over an hour. Early that afternoon Operation Dynamo ended.

Twelve days later the *Lady of Mann* was in action once more. She became part of the force of personnel ships assigned to Operation Ariel, the evacuation from the ports of north-west France. She was at Le Havre, Cherbourg and Brest, embarking troops as the enemy advanced in a vast encircling movement. She was one of the last three ships to leave Le Havre and it was estimated that she had 5,000 troops on board as she pulled out under air attack.

From the following August until April, 1944, the *Lady of Mann* did troop transport duties, mainly between Invergordon, Aberdeen and Lerwick and to the Faroes. At times she was also engaged ferrying troops and Air Force personnel from the *Queen Mary*, which served throughout the war as a trooper. The *Queen* would come into Belfast from Canada or the United States, turn round quickly and set off again westwards. The Steam Packet Company ship was one of several that serviced the big Cunarder, taking the troops on the final leg of their sea voyage to Greenock.

The *Lady of Mann* was then taken over by the Admiralty and converted to an LSI (H) — a Landing Ship Infantry (Hand Hoisting). She carried six landing assault craft, 55 officers and 435 men.

On D-Day, June 6, 1944, she was the headquarters ship of the senior officer of the 512th Assault Flotilla, responsible for the landings in the Juno area near Courselles.

Later in the month, while still on the Normandy operations, she was retired for repairs and then went back to her duties as a personnel vessel. She served as such for the remainder of the war, carrying on for some months afterwards moving troops and bringing out displaced persons. She was mostly in the Channel plying to Ostende and the Hook from such ports as Dover and Harwich.

She returned to Douglas on March 9, 1946, when she was given a civic reception. A local paper that week said that during her war service the *Lady of Mann* had carried more than 2,000,000 troops.

Two months later she was reconditioned and she returned to the Steam Packet Company.

Ben-my-Chree (IV) on war service in the English Channel.

The *Ben-my-Chree* (IV) was requisitioned a few days after the outbreak of war and served as a personnel ship until she was released in May 1946.

On the night of June 2, 1940, she was damaged when she came into collision with another ship soon after leaving Folkestone for Dunkirk. This finished her involvement in the operation but she had already rescued 4,095 troops and brought them to England. Her Master was Captain G. Woods.

She then worked on transport duties between northern British ports and Iceland until the beginning of 1944. During these voyages she earned a reputation as a good sea boat, and was sometimes able to keep her station while naval vessels around her were falling back in heavy weather.

The *Ben* was then prepared as a Landing Ship Infantry (Hand Hoisting) vessel with a carrying capacity of six landing craft. At the opening of the D-Day campaign she was in action off the famous Omaha beach. She was the headquarters ship of the Senior Officer of the 514th Assault Flotilla and she carried U.S. Rangers.

When her duty in the great invasion was completed the *Ben* was employed on the cross-Channel transport service until released for reconditioning in May, 1946. She was returned to the Steam Packet Company a month later.

Victoria landed British and U.S. troops in Normandy.

The war service of one Steam Packet Company vessel attracted much less attention than that of the others. This was the *Victoria*, generally regarded as having spent the war years plying from Douglas, at first to Liverpool and then to Fleetwood. This she did for much of the time, but she was on decidedly active service as well.

She was the only Company ship to be mined in the Irish Sea. This occurred on December 27, 1940, when she was homeward bound with passengers from Liverpool, under Captain John Keig. She was holed by a magnetic mine when North-west of the Bar Light.

Some of her passengers, of whom there were more than 200, were taken off by the trawler *Yulan*, and taken on to Douglas and landed safely. Others were returned to Liverpool by the Pilot Boat. The *Victoria* was towed back to Liverpool. There were no casualties, but the incident had important consequences for the Company.

The *Victoria* was later fitted out as an LSI (H) after her mine damage had been repaired, and she then worked out of the Firth of Forth as a target vessel.

After an overhaul in Leith and service from Dundee she was ordered to Southampton in the summer of 1943, where she was employed on training infantry for the forthcoming assault on Europe. She did this work for some months, mainly under the Portland Command, practising landings. It was unspectacular, repetitive work, but it was of immense value, and scores of smaller ships from the merchant navy were involved.

On D-Day, June 6, 1944, the *Victoria* was one of the vessels scheduled to land assault forces on the western extreme of the small bay of Arromanches, which was one of the three British

Army spearheads into France. They landed successfully. Unluckily, as happened elsewhere on the front on that momentous day, a German flak-ship on routine anti-invasion exercise was in the Bay and was able to produce superior fire power to the wave of assault craft that proceeded ashore. Nevertheless, despite losses, the bridgehead held and Arromanches soon became famous for one of the successful artificial harbours built so hurriedly to sustain the foothold of the armies.

At the time the *Victoria*'s crew had Steam Packet Company men as officers, and she continued to fly the Red Ensign with John Keig in command. To the Admiralty she was a mongrel; her landing assault craft were manned by naval men whose officers were mainly R.N.V.R.

Later for some days the *Victoria* landed American assault forces on Utah beach, where difficult resistance had been encountered. She then proceeded to service the harbour at Arromanches, landing troops and supplies.

As the war moved east, she reverted to the work of a personnel carrier. She became something of an emergency hospital ship, lifting sick and wounded and moving them mainly to shore based hospitals around Dieppe. When not doing this work the ship was carrying troops back on leave to Britain.

*   *   *

On the home front the Company's war work fell into three phases. The first was the maintenance of the lifeline between Douglas and Liverpool, which had endured week in and week out, summer and winter, for over a hundred years. It had been an outstanding service to the community, and was appreciated as such by the Manx. Over several months of the year it was kept going for very meagre returns. The work was always highly seasonal and the heavy summer traffic was needed to make up for the much reduced winter trade. It was a pattern to which the Company had been accustomed for many years.

From the start of the war two ships, at first the *Victoria* and *Rushen Castle*, were able to maintain the daily passenger service, with one ship leaving Douglas at nine in the morning — which remains the traditional departure time from the island — and the other leaving Liverpool usually at around 10.45 hours. Minefields were laid by the Royal Navy around the approaches to the Mersey as a protection against enemy submarines, and Steam Packet Company captains would be given orders how to proceed. No Company ship was torpedoed on the Irish Sea run throughout the war.

The passenger complement on these voyages consisted mainly of service personnel travelling to the island for training or on leave, small groups of internees, and civilians on essential business. The journeys were not always simple, and were sometimes prolonged; congestion in the Mersey as war traffic built up in the port area of Liverpool could cause long delays. But the general impression from the records in the Company's sailing sheets is that the service worked remarkably well, even through the abnormally hard winter of early 1940.

The second phase in the war as far as the home run was concerned occurred gradually, starting at the time of the overrunning of the Low Countries leading up to the distant withdrawal from Dunkirk. The first sign of these events was in the sudden appearance in Manx waters of the Belgian cross-Channel steamer the *Princess Josephine Charlotte*.

At the collapse of Belgium a number of cross-Channel ships were in Ostend harbour and the Belgians filled them with refugees and sent them to England, where the vessels were taken over by the authorities. The *Princess* was sent to Liverpool and from there she made four trips to the Island, three of them to Douglas and one to Ramsey, bringing with her what the Steam Packet Company's sailing list laconically listed as "females", without even specifying the numbers.

These women were aliens, due for internment. Most of them were taken across the island to Port Erin, where the women internees were mostly housed. They were the first sign, to the Manx, that Britain was taking final precautions against the possibility of invasion.

The Belgian ship left Manx waters after one week, and was not met again by the Company's ships until the D-Day landings on Normandy. One other Belgian steamer appeared at Douglas even more briefly.

On Tuesday, June 4, the *Victoria* arrived at Douglas with 401 aliens. Four days later the *Snaefell* brought 267 females. Then from Tuesday, June 11 to Friday the 14th the *Rushen Castle* made three round trips to Liverpool, returning with a total of 3,022 aliens. The *Rushen Castle* appeared to be the chief ship for this work, and on the 22nd she brought in 1,197 internees. This traffic then dwindled, although smaller numbers were recorded from time to time for some months.

As the summer progressed so difficulties of another type occurred on the home run. The Port of Liverpool was now often closed, usually for half a day. The reasons were not at first given; it could have been magnetic mines dropped in the channel during the night, or sheer congestion in the docks. But on September 27 comes the first reference in the sailing lists to yet another reason; the Coburg dock had been bombed. The Company's only loss was 35 tons of cargo, waiting to be loaded. It was destroyed by fire.

The bombing of Liverpool docks increased in severity. Towards the end of October the port was often closed, and Company ships would sometimes be ordered to anchor at the Bar for up to 24 hours before proceeding. In the last week of the month one of the Company's sheds at No. 5 dock received a direct hit, killing a watchman and 30 dockers and burying 200 tons of waiting cargo. Yet still the transport of troops, naval and R.A.F. personnel and aliens continued. The alien intake seldom exceeded 200 a voyage and was sometimes a mere dozen or two. The eventual total, however, went into thousands.

November and early December of that vital year were marked by heavy gales; the weather was so bad that on two occasions sailings had to be cancelled, an extreme rarity even in wartime. The air raids were spasmodic but heavy, culminating in severe bombings on Liverpool on the Friday and Saturday before Christmas. The port was closed for two days and the *Victoria* next crossed to Fleetwood.

The climax came on the day after Boxing Day, when the *Victoria* was mined after leaving Liverpool.

Within a matter of days the Steam Packet Company had switched its route. From then on it plied between Douglas and Fleetwood. It continued this trade until April 6, 1946, after which it returned to Liverpool for the main crossing.

The Fleetwood alternative run was the third phase of the war on the Company's home schedule. It occupied most of the war and was mainly uneventful, although it was strictly supervised by the transport and naval authorities.

* * *

It could be said that the men of the Steam Packet Company received only meagre recognition for their work during the evacuation of the French ports in 1940 and the assault on Normandy on D-Day in 1944.

However that may be, Captain T. C. Woods of the *Lady of Mann* was later awarded an O.B.E. Captain R. Duggan of the *Mona's Queen* was awarded the Distinguished Service Cross and the ship's bo'sun E. Watterson the Distinguished Service Medal.

Three D.S.C.'s were awarded to the *Tynwald*, one of them to the radio officer who was a Marconi Company man and not a member of the Steam Packet Company. Captain J. H.

Whiteway and the Chief Officer A. Watterson were both awarded the D.S.C., and A/B Seaman T. Gribben the D.S.M.

The Purser of the *Viking*, E. H. Bishop, was awarded the D.S.C.

Several other officers and crew were awarded medals or Mentioned in Dispatches.

And so the war ended, and the Steam Packet Company ships that had survived returned slowly to their home port. They had a remarkably good record. They had seen service in the great evacuation from Dunkirk and on the many ports in northern France and even down into the Bay of Biscay. They had worked as transports as far north as Iceland. They had helped in the evacuation of the Channel Islands and done duty in the Mediterranean.

When D-Day came they played their part in the return to mainland Europe. After that, they helped to keep the lifelines going to the invasion forces.

Their finest statistic has perhaps not been sufficiently emphasised. Eight of the Company's ships took part in the evacuation from Dunkirk, two under the White Ensign, and six as merchantmen. Between them they brought out 24,669 troops.

Winston Churchill in his *History of the Second World War* gave the total number of British and Allied Troops landed in England from Dunkirk as 338,226.

It is a fair record that one man in every 14 saved was brought out in a Steam Packet Company ship registered in Douglas.

CHAPTER EIGHT: *A Flying Interlude*

FOR TWELVE YEARS, STARTING BETWEEN THE
two World Wars, the Steam Packet Company had a direct interest in commercial air
transport as a part-proprietor of one of the many small airlines which were formed in those
pioneering days. As always, it was cautious, but it was prepared to join with the old London,
Midland and Scottish Railway as a partner in Railway Air Services, which operated a freight
service.

At the time many companies, employing a variety of types of aircraft, were calling at the
Isle of Man. Nearly all the schedules were for the summer only, and Railway Air Services,
having started on August 20, 1934 stopped running for the year on September 29.

The following year, on April 15, 1935, it became The Manx Airway and started operating
a passenger service on a route from Manchester-Liverpool-Blackpool-Ronaldsway. The
route was highly successful for its day, 5,675 passengers and 40 tons of freight being carried in
the first season.

There was considerable expansion the following year, 1936. A service from Manchester to
Belfast was organised with stops at Liverpool and Ronaldsway. It operated twice a day on
weekdays in winter, three times daily from April to September, with two Sunday services
during the April-September season. Several other routes were operated, linking Ronaldsway
with Glasgow and Leeds among other places. De Havilland Rapides and Dragons were the
aircraft used. It was an ambitious programme.

In his annual report to the shareholders meeting in February, 1937, the Chairman admitted
that the enterprise had lost money on the year, but he was able to assure members that the
basic agreement with the L.M.S. put a limit to the loss borne by the shipping company.

The Steam Packet Company's air interests continued to expand in 1937 against the general
pattern of the domestic British air business, which was in serious need of rationalisation.
Competition was so excessive that scarcely a single carrier was making any sort of a profit.
This did not deter The Manx Airway. More routes were operated than the previous year, in
some cases with greater frequency. The southern penetration went as far as London, but all
services were withdrawn from the end of September.

Throughout the 1937 summer it had been more than ever obvious that air routes to any
part of the mainland could only be made profitable if the number of competing operators was
reduced.

The rational development was the formation of Isle of Man Air Services Limited, a
combination of the three main contractors, the L.M.S., the Steam Packet Company, and Olley
Air Services. The third of these companies had behind it a complex of influential backers.
Captain G. P. Olley had been one of the pioneer pilots of Imperial Airways.

The capital of the new Manx company was £75,000, with the three different interests each
contributing £25,000. All three would provide two directors apiece, and each partner would

INTER-AVAILABILITY OF TICKETS.

Air, to return Rail and/or Steamer.

If you hold a return ticket and for any reason wish to travel back by surface transport you can, provided reasonable notice of cancellation has been given, exchange the return half of your air ticket at a railway booking office for a first-class single ticket available by any recognised direct railway and/or steamship route back to the place from which you started.

Passengers returning by any indirect route will be allowed the amount due on the unused portion of the Air ticket towards the cost of surface travel.

By arrangement, the services of the Belfast Steamship Company, Burns & Laird Lines, the Isle of Man Steam Packet Company, may be used in addition to the railway companies' steamships.

Rail and/or Steamer to return by Air.

If you have taken your outward journey by surface transport and hold the return half of an Ordinary, Tourist, Monthly Return, Week-end or Holiday rail and/or steamer ticket, you may, on handing in the return half of your surface ticket return by air or combination of air and surface transport, on payment of an appropriate supplement.

In the case of children, the published air fare must be paid, and you can apply to the railway company for a refund on the unused portion of the railway ticket.

GENERAL CONDITIONS OF CARRIAGE.

The conditions under which the carriage of passengers and baggage is undertaken are displayed at any Isle of Man Air Services' booking office or at the Airports, and are printed on the back of the Air ticket.

Every endeavour will be made to maintain the advertised Schedule, but the Company cannot accept responsibility for delay or cancellation due to weather or other conditions, and it is not possible to guarantee connections between services.

DEPARTURES.

You want to avoid trouble and confusion at the last moment, and so do we, and we ask, therefore, that you arrive at the Departure Booking Office or Airport about ten minutes previous to the advertised time of departure of the service, so that we can deal with the embarkation formalities and give you any other assistance you may require.

ISLE of MAN AIR SERVICES Ltd.

Advance 1938 Spring and Summer
TIME TABLE

Liable to Alteration without previous notice being given. For fuller Details and Fares not quoted, apply to your nearest Travel Agent, Railway Station, or—

ISLE OF MAN.
I.O.M. Airport. Tel., Castletown 106/7.
L.M.S., Parade St., Douglas. Tel., Douglas 567.
I.O.M. Steam Packet, Douglas. Tel., Douglas 1101.

LONDON.
Euston House, Seymour St., N.W.1. Tel., Euston 1234; Ext. 640.
Airway Terminus, Victoria Station, S.W.1. Tel., Victoria 2211.
Olley Air Services, Ltd., Airport of London, Croydon. Tel., Croydon 5117.

LEEDS.
Wellington Station. Tel. 31211.

LIVERPOOL.
Speke Airport. Tel., Garston 848.
Lime St. Station. Tel., Royal 2960; Ext. 61.

BLACKPOOL.
Stanley Park Aerodrome. Tel., Blackpool 4020.
Central Station. Tel. 1243.

BRADFORD.
Forster Sq. Station. Tel. 4826.

MANCHESTER.
L.M.S. Office, 47, Piccadilly. Tel., Central 0384.
Air Services. Tel., Eccles 1392.

BELFAST.
York Road Station. Tel. 44211.
11, Donegal Place. Tel. 44211.

CARLISLE.
Carlisle Airport. Tel., Carlisle 1651.
Central Station. Tel. 1340; Ext. 38.

GLASGOW.
Renfrew Aerodrome. Tel., Renfrew 230.
Central Station. Tel., Douglas 2900.

RESERVATIONS.
Seats should be booked in advance for either forward or Return journeys and reservations may be made at any office named above.

FARES AND FREIGHT RATES.

Isle of Man To and From—	Single.	Return.	Mid-Week Return.	Freight per lb.
Belfast	27/6	45/-	40/-	3d.
Blackpool	30/-	50/-	45/-	3d.
Carlisle	30/-	50/-	45/-	3d.
Glasgow (direct)	40/-	75/-	65/-	4d.
Liverpool	32/6	55/-	50/-	3d.
Leeds/Bradford	50/-	80/-	70/-	4d.
Manchester	37/6	63/-	55/-	3d.

MID-WEEK FARES, available outward on Tuesday, Wednesday and Thursday only, and for return on any Tuesday, Wednesday or Thursday within one month from date of outward journey. Passengers may return on any Friday, Saturday, Sunday or Monday within three months on payment of the difference between the midweek return and the ordinary return fare.

BOOKINGS.

You can reserve your seat and buy your ticket at any Station or Agency of the British Railways, or if you wish it at the particular address shown in this time table.

Accommodation in the aircraft is limited and we must ask you, therefore, to book in advance for either the forward or return journey.

BAGGAGE.

Each passenger is allowed 35 lbs of personal baggage free of charge. No free baggage is allowed to children travelling at half-fares or travelling free. Baggage in excess of the free allowance—Air Freight Rates. (Minimum charge not made.)

AVAILABILITY OF AIR TICKETS.

Ordinary Return tickets are valid for three calendar months from the date of the outward journey. If you want to break your journey at any place en route you should advise the booking office who will issue sectional tickets at the sectional fares, and reserve accordingly.

SPRING TIME TABLE (1938) — MARCH 28th to MAY 31st inclusive.

	WEEKDAYS.							SUNDAYS.		
	a.m.	a.m.	a.m.	p.m.	p.m.	A p.m.	A p.m.	a.m.	p.m.	p.m.
ISLE OF MAN .... dep.	8-0	9-0	9-15	2-45	5-0	5-10	6-10	11-0	12-15	2-15
BLACKPOOL .... arr.	—	—	9-50	—	5-35	—	—	11-35	—	2-50
BLACKPOOL .... dep.	—	—	10-0	—	5-45	—	—	11-45	—	3-0
LIVERPOOL .... arr.	8-45	—	10-15	3-30	6-0	5-55	—	12-0	—	3-15
LIVERPOOL .... dep.	9-0	—	10-25	3-40	—	—	—	12-10	—	—
MANCHESTER .... arr.	9-15	—	10-40	3-55	—	—	—	12-25	—	—
BELFAST .... arr.	—	9-30	—	—	—	—	6-40	—	12-45	—
	a.m.	a.m.	p.m.	p.m.	A p.m.	A p.m.	p.m.	a.m.	p.m.	p.m.
BELFAST .... dep.	—	—	2-0	—	4-30	—	—	—	1-30	—
MANCHESTER .... dep.	—	10-50	—	2-15	—	4-50	—	—	—	2-0
LIVERPOOL .... arr.	—	11-5	—	2-30	—	—	5-5	—	—	2-15
LIVERPOOL .... dep.	8-0	11-20	—	2-45	—	5-15	5-15	11-0	—	2-25
BLACKPOOL .... arr.	—	11-35	—	—	—	—	5-30	11-15	—	2-40
BLACKPOOL .... dep.	—	11-45	—	—	—	—	5-40	11-25	—	2-50
ISLE OF MAN .... arr.	8-45	12-20	2-30	3-30	5-0	6-0	6-15	12-0	2-0	3-25

A—Operates only from May 23rd.

SUMMER TIME TABLE (1938) — JUNE 1st to SEPTEMBER 10th inclusive.
ENGLAND and ISLE OF MAN.

	N S a.m.	N S a.m.	N S a.m.	a.m.	a.m.	p.m.	p m.	p.m.	p.m.	A N S p.m.	B p.m.
ISLE OF MAN .... dep.	—	8-0	9-15	10-20	11-30	12-45	2-45	3-10	5-0	5-10	6-45
BLACKPOOL .... arr.	—	—	9-50	—	12-5	—	—	3-45	5-35	—	7-20
BLACKPOOL .... dep.	—	—	10-0	—	12-15	—	—	3-55	5-45	—	7-30
LIVERPOOL .... arr.	—	8-45	10-15	11-5	—	1-30	3-30	4-10	6-0	5-55	7-45
LIVERPOOL .... dep.	8-0	9-0	10-25	11-15	—	1-40	3-40	4-20	6-10	—	—
MANCHESTER .... arr.	8-15	9-15	10-40	11-30	—	1-55	—	4-35	6-25	—	—
LEEDS & BRADFORD .... arr.	—	—	—	—	12-45	—	4-10	—	—	—	—
	N S a.m.	a.m.	N S a.m.	a.m.	noon	p.m.	p.m.	p.m.	A N S p.m.	p.m.	p.m.
LEEDS & BRADFORD .... dep.		N S		—	—	1-5	—	4-35	—	—	—
MANCHESTER .... dep.	—	8-30	9-45	10-50	12-0	—	2-15	—	—	5-45	6-45
LIVERPOOL .... arr.	—	8-45	10-0	11-5	12-15	—	2-30	5-5	—	6-0	7-0
LIVERPOOL .... dep.	8-0	8-55	10-10	11-20	12-25	—	2-45	5-15	5-15	6-10	—
BLACKPOOL .... arr.	—	—	10-25	11-35	—	1-35	—	5-30	—	6-25	—
BLACKPOOL .... dep.	—	—	10-35	11-45	—	1-45	—	5-40	—	6-35	—
ISLE OF MAN .... arr.	8-45	9-40	11-10	12-20	1-10	2-20	3-30	6-15	6-0	7-10	—

CARLISLE and ISLE OF MAN.

	a.m.	c p.m.
ISLE OF MAN .... dep.	11-15	3-15
CARLISLE .... arr.	12-0	4-0
	p.m.	c p.m.
CARLISLE .... dep.	1-0	4-15
ISLE OF MAN .... arr.	1-45	5-0

BELFAST and ISLE OF MAN.

	a.m.	c p.m.	A N S p.m.
ISLE OF MAN .... dep.	9-0	3-0	6-10
BELFAST .... arr.	9-35	3-35	6-40
	a.m.	c p.m.	A N S p.m.
BELFAST .... dep.	9-50	3-50	4-30
ISLE OF MAN .... arr.	10-25	4-25	5-0

GLASGOW and ISLE OF MAN.

	a.m.	a.m.	p.m.
ISLE OF MAN .... dep.	8-40	11-30	5-0
GLASGOW .... arr.	9-45	12-35	6-5
	a.m.	p.m.	p.m.
GLASGOW .... dep.	10-0	12-50	6-20
ISLE OF MAN .... arr.	11-5	1-55	7-25

EXPLANATIONS.

A—Operates until September 3rd.
B—15 Minutes earlier from September 4th.
C—Daily, Sundays included, from July 1st.
N S—Not Sundays.

For Fares and Booking Office Addresses, see reverse side.

supply the chairman in rotation for two years at a time. The advantages were obvious: money would be saved in cutting out the duplication of overheads; there would be a better deal for the travelling public and a chance of a profit to the owners.

The years 1938-1939 were poor ones for the domestic air services. The slump of the 1930's still lingered, surplus spending power was low and unemployment high.

Nevertheless in 1938 Isle of Man Air Services did succeed in one of its main ambitions. At the end of the summer season it was granted provisional route licences from the Secretary of State for Air which placed it in the position of exclusive carrier to and from the Island with the exception of the Dublin route, and one daily summer call on the Belfast-Croydon route. This licence gave the Company part of the British Government's new subsidy for internal air routes.

All civilian flying was suspended when war broke out on September 3, 1939, but limited scale flights between Ronaldsway and Liverpool and Ronaldsway and Belfast were restored at the end of November. The war had almost ended before the blackout, imposed for security reasons, was removed from the windows of the planes.

During the war changes took place in the share structure of the air company. 12,500 shares were transferred from Olley to the Steam Packet Company, which then had 37,500 shares or half the capital.

A year after the war ended British European Airways was formed and it took over the Isle of Man Air Services on February 1, 1947. On February 26 Mr. J. F. Crellin presided at the Steam Packet Company's annual general meeting and said there had been every reason to expect a future of profitable development in their air interests. But once the British Government had decided to take over all internal air services the Company accepted that a small unit had little or no chance of competing with B.E.A.

The Steam Packet Company was reimbursed to the full cost of the shares with which it had backed the air venture, and it also received £8,300 as a small premium. This was all it could expect from the nationalisation decision. As a Manx company, of course, it had been outside the United Kingdom, but at that time it could not hope to run a successful air line into U.K. airports.

In 13 years of operation Isle of Man Air Services had carried 137,359 passengers, had handled £2,700,000 of mail, and £600,000 of freight. All this without loss of life.

In 1956 efforts were made to persuade the Steam Packet Company to join a syndicate that, had it succeeded in getting a licence, could have operated a service connecting the Island at least with Liverpool. There was immediate opposition from B.E.A. and the idea was dropped. At the 1957 annual meeting the Steam Packet Chairman said that non-participation need be no cause for regret, as little if any profit appeared to be forthcoming. He was probably correct.

Meanwhile there was a steady increase in air travel. By the mid 1960's incoming air traffic to the Island exceeded 200,000 passengers a year, thus creaming off some business from the shipping company. There were 205,043 arrivals at Ronaldsway Airport in 1966. The figures have faltered somewhat in recent years, again perhaps emphasising the changing British holiday habits. In 1977 the arrivals by air totalled 176,411 and the 1978 figure was 186,271.

CHAPTER NINE: *Round the Clock*

THE DAILY ROUTINE ON AN ISLE OF MAN STEAM Packet passenger ship very obviously depends on the time of year. The size of the crews varies according to the season, the catering staff being much fewer in winter. In summer the crews expect to work substantially long hours, during which they earn considerable overtime pay and build up a credit in subsequent leave.

The Company's car ferries have certificates to carry a crew of approximately 60, comprising: Captain, Chief Officer, Second Officer, Radio Officer, a Chief, Second and two Third engineering officers, a bo'sun and 11 seamen, a donkeyman and up to seven other engine room hands, one electrician and one ship's carpenter. These thirty positions do not vary throughout the year.

The catering staff is flexible. At its maximum it could consist of: Chief Steward, Second Steward, Captain's Steward, up to five lounge stewards, four dining saloon stewards, First cook, Second cook, Crew's cook, two galley boys, first and second pantrymen, two pantry boys, two barmen, two bar boys, two stewardesses, up to six women buffet assistants and up to six trainee boys.

All the senior catering staff are permanent employees; the juniors are usually engaged on a seasonal basis. In practice the catering staff would not be crewed to the maximum of each of these groups. With the full complement of officers, seamen and engineering staff the greatest number of other staff at any one time would be 31.

The crews of the Company's cargo ships, *Peveril* (III) and *Conister* (II) vary comparatively little throughout the year. The six passenger vessels have sailing schedules that differ widely during the summer. A fair indication of work aboard a car ferry in the busy season on a daily return run to Liverpool — in contrast to the winter, when she would almost certainly go out to Liverpool one day and back the next — is as follows:

There would be little sign of activity in the early hours at the berth in Douglas Harbour as the night watchman goes on his traditional rounds, alert against the sudden appearance of strangers on the quayside or gangway. No one is allowed on board without authorisation. The watchman himself is a seaman, a member of the crew, all the sailors taking the duty in turn.

With the ship berthed alongside the pier overnight, power and lighting are kept to a minimum, being supplied by means of a mains cable from the shore. A duty engineer will be sleeping aboard and will be available in any emergency. There will be at least one duty officer aboard, and almost certainly the Master if the weather reports are at all unfavourable. A number of crew members will be asleep in their quarters. The days of the fo'castle are long gone: regulations provide for cabins for all crew.

One of the night watchmen's early morning duties is to break out the ship's flags, which will have been lowered at nightfall. Up will go the ensign and the name flag, the house flag and stem jack, together with the Blue Peter. The day has started.

For the crew activity begins at 0600 hours; the donkeyman will come on duty and preparations will start for the nine o'clock sailing to Liverpool. At 0630 hours the Chief and Second Steward are called by the night watchman and the Second then proceeds to call the cooks, pantrymen, and catering staff. The business of preparing the first meal of the day goes ahead at once and the sailing staff take breakfast at seven, the catering staff in relays.

Meanwhile the donkeyman will have carried out his first job of the day. The ship's own alternators are started, the power link with the shore is wound in and the donkeyman, who is responsible for the auxiliary services, will go round the electrical distribution boxes and close lighting and heating switches to enable power to be switched on in the lounges, car decks and private cabins, which will have been in darkness overnight. The second generator will then be started and deck machinery circuit breakers will be activated so that the seamen can single in the mooring ropes. This enables the ship to be manoeuvred into the loading position so that the car ramp and passenger gangways can be positioned at precisely the right points. Down in the engine room pumps and heaters will be started up in order to warm the main engines and thus prepare for departure. At this time an engineer will be checking and testing the machinery and the electrician will check to see that all electrical equipment is in order.

This routine will differ in a turbine driven ship, where preparations for the voyage will start with the warming up of the fuel oil bringing it up to about 220°F., after which the donkeyman will "flash up" the two main boilers to raise steam. At 0745 he will disconnect the turning gear on the propeller shafts and will start the main engine's lubrication pumps.

The catering staff will have had a routine of their own. They will have prepared their various services, laying up tables in dining saloon and lounges, seeing to brass and silver and so on. The catering boys will have drawn galley, pantry, buffet or dining saloon requirements from the stores. Fresh foodstuffs, such as milk, bread and meat, will be delivered from the quayside.

The mail is the first of the morning's cargo to go aboard. Parcel mail is stowed on the shelter deck, while letter mail is taken down and locked in its own special mail room at the after end of the car deck. Punctually at 0800 hours all staff stand by their duty points in readiness for the arrival of the passengers. The Chief and Second stewards inspect all passenger accommodation. Cooks and pantrymen prepare breakfasts; fresh sandwiches for the buffets are made and wrapped before each trip. Luncheon for passengers and officers is prepared and is served from 1100 hours until arrival at destination point.

On a steam driven turbine ship like the *Ben-my-Chree* the third engineer will go below punctually at 0800 and ensure that everything is working smoothly. He will open the main steam cocks and signal the donkeyman to ease open the steam valves on the boilers. After a series of operations the propeller shafts will start turning at about 5 r.p.m. to make sure that the turbines are warming up correctly.

Passengers and vehicles will now be coming aboard, their tickets being checked at the gangways. During the hour before departure the ship's carpenter in conjunction with the engineers will check the main helm and steering gear, and the bow rudder steering gear.

Approximately five minutes before sailing the ship's siren sounds and the car ramp will be withdrawn. The seamen make ready for leaving port. In the engine room of the motor vessels the engineer on duty will have started the main engines and the clutches will be engaged; the two propeller shafts will be turning slowly. The bow thrust drive which aids the vessel in manoeuvering will be started up.

About two minutes before 9 o'clock the telegraph rings from the bridge to the engine room: "Stand by". Up to this point the main engines are in direct control of the engineers in the engine control room, but on "stand by" the telegraph control is changed over to the bridge when the Master now has direct control of the engine speed and propeller pitch.

At 0900 the passenger gangway is taken in and the order is received to let go fore and aft. There will be three heavy blasts on the ship's whistle and the ship moves slowly astern.

The Captain is always in personal command taking the ship out from cast off to clear — that is, from the time the vessel starts moving astern from its berth until it is on course. The Second Officer always takes the helm during this series of operations. Engines are now put to full ahead and the course is set for the Liverpool Bar 54 miles away.

After leaving port the Master hands over to the Duty Officer, who is responsible for navigating the vessel. A seaman takes the helm from the Second Officer and a second seaman remains on the bridge as a lookout. During the crossing the Captain can be alerted immediately by a telephone line from the bridge to his cabin.

Down in the engine control room the engineers on duty will be watching the pressures and temperature readings, and the greasers will be keeping the machinery under constant observation. If weather conditions are adverse the stabilisers will be brought into use. All this time the dining saloon stewards are serving breakfasts and from 1100 hours, lunches.

During the crossing the radio officer, who is not a Steam Packet man but who belongs to one of the marine radio organisations, will be at his transmitter to keep in touch with Anglesey Radio. The journey up the Channel to Prince's Landing Stage at Liverpool takes just under an hour. During this time the vessel is under the pilotage of the Master. All Steam Packet Captains and some Chief Officers carry pilot's certificates for the Mersey, Lower Clyde, Belfast and Fleetwood. The Dublin authorities provide their own pilots. Once a master or officer has gained his pilot's licence for these ports he has it renewed yearly. This does not involve him in further examinations providing he can claim the necessary number of journeys in and out of the port concerned.

Once alongside Prince's Landing Stage, engine control changes over from the bridge to the engine room by a signal on the ship's telegraph. The crew will then have approximately 2½ hours in which to disembark passengers and vehicles, clean ship and reload for the return journey. Any fresh stores required are taken aboard and the staff, who have been lunching in relays, get a short break in which to freshen up for the second spell of duty. The ship, if she is making the afternoon sailing, traditionally returns at 1530 hours.

If fuel oil is to be loaded, the Second Engineer and greasers will attend to the business of getting it on board from the bunker barge which ties up alongside. The oil-fired turbine driven vessels burn up about 20 tons a round trip, but the diesels are more economical, burning about 10 tons. While in port the donkeyman, who has been off duty since the ship cast off from Douglas, will be back at work attending to such machinery as is needed, filling service tanks and so on. With bunkering complete, passengers and vehicles can once again come aboard for the voyage back to Douglas. Loading usually starts at 1430 hours when the staff once more stand by their duty posts.

Afternoon tea is served in the dining saloon from 1500 hours, followed by a high tea service which begins at 1600 hours. Bars and buffet service carry on throughout the trip until shortly before the vessel arrives in port, usually at 1900 hours or shortly after. During both outward and inward trips the staff have a relief system for their own meals.

The engines will be restarted as departure time from Liverpool nears, and their control will once again change over to the bridge, where the Master is in personal command of the vessel until the Bar is reached.

In summer, there are midnight sailings in both directions on certain nights. To the crew the routine is almost exactly the same. The ship leaves Douglas at its scheduled time and is alongside at Liverpool at about 0400 hours. Her stay in port after her turn round is mostly rather longer than in the case of the traditional 0900 sailing, for she usually picks up passengers and vehicles and leaves for the return journey at about 1100 when once again main meals are served.

Shortly before arriving at Douglas the vessel will receive berthing instructions from the Harbourmaster including the numbers of the car and gangway doors which are to be used for disembarkation. The Captain will be back on the Bridge. Before reaching the pier the seamen put out the fenders for berthing the ship and the usual drill for tying up is then followed. The main engines and auxiliary machinery will be stopped if the vessel is to remain in its home port overnight. The duty engineer and donkeyman will once again change over to shore power and the ship's generators will be stopped until morning. There will still be a certain amount of work for the catering staff who will change into working clothes and do the main cleaning of the public areas, leaving the dusting and polishing until the following morning when they start a similar day.

With nightfall the flags come down, the night watchman is on duty, and the ship's crew is either ashore or in quarters afloat. It has been an uneventful but busy day.

―――――――――

This chapter concludes with a pictorial description of a sailing from Douglas to Liverpool and back. At the request of the author and with the co-operation of the Steam Packet Co. (who kindly gave him the "run of the ship") Mr. W.S. Basnett made the journey and took the photographs which follow.

―――――――――

The watchman is on duty and the donkeyman starts up the generator.

The deserted car deck ready for the motorists to embark.

The duty engineer in the engine control room.

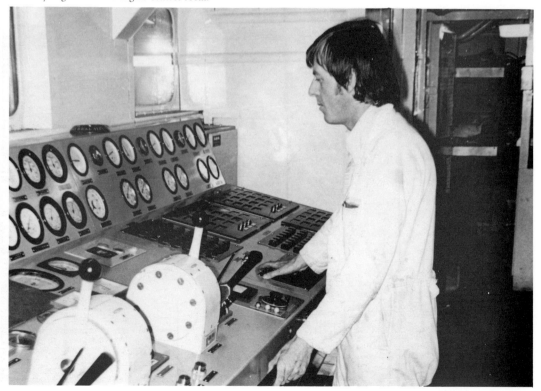

The *Lady of Mann* has two main lounges (above and below), a ladies lounge, two smoke rooms and sleeping accommodation. There are also private cabins (facing page) which offer every comfort particularly on a night crossing.

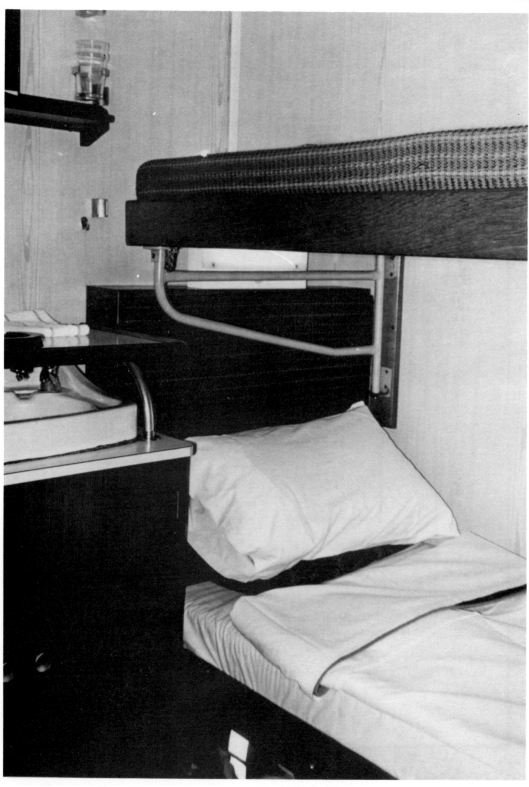

Cars assemble on the King Edward VIII Pier (one of the few reminders of this monarch's brief reign).

Returning holidaymakers receive a cheery word from Purser Callin Hudson as he collects their tickets.

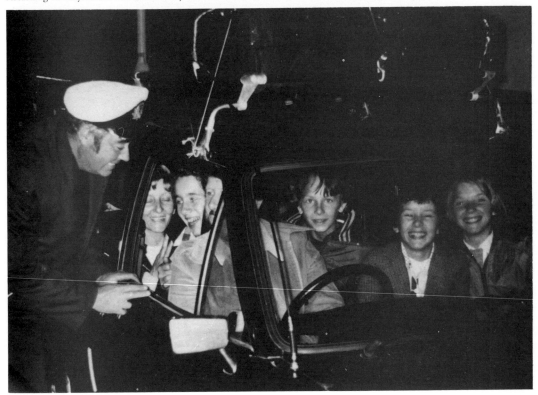

Returning holidaymakers board the ship by the passenger gangway and at midnight the vessel sails for Liverpool.

Helmsman George Wilson takes his turn at the wheel.

About 4 a.m. Capt. J. S. Kennaugh, Commodore of the Isle of Man Steam Packet Co. brings the *Lady of Mann* up the Mersey to the Prince's Landing Stage.

While in Liverpool perishable foodstuffs such as bread, milk and vegetables are brought aboard and an hour before sailing time embarkation begins.

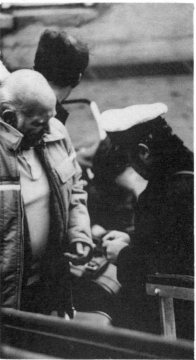

Nearly 9 o'clock by the Liver Building clock and the *Lady of Mann* leaves again for Douglas.

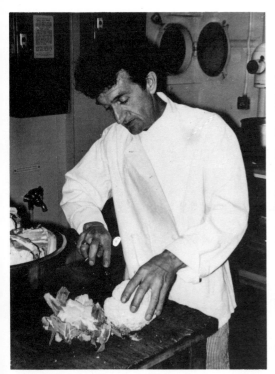

Both breakfast and lunch have to be cooked and served on this crossing. Here we see vegetables being prepared and a dining saloon steward laying a table.

Capt. Kennaugh brings the *Lady of Mann* into Douglas Harbour to berth alongside the King Edward Pier and another round trip to Liverpool is over.

CHAPTER TEN: *Behind the Flag*

Flags SPEAK THEIR OWN LANGUAGE TO SEAMEN everywhere as well as to those specialist enthusiasts who delight in calling themselves vexillologists. These are the flag collectors and students: the first part of their strange and not very felicitous name is based on the Latin *vexillarius*, a Roman standard bearer, carrier of the vexillum or flag.

The Steam Packet Company's house flag is red, with the three-legged symbol of the Isle of Man in the centre, and the initials of the Company, IOMSPC, arranged equally and horizontally on either side of the symbol.

The most interesting, and at one time the most provocative flag flown on the Company's vessels, is the Manx variant of the Red Ensign, with the three-legged symbol of the island on the red background in the fly of the flag.

The Three Legs of Man are of great age; their origin is probably pagan and certainly obscure. The symbol has been carried on Steam Packet Company ships over the last 150 years, being built in at the time of construction, usually on the stern, but sometimes on the bows or elsewhere as well. Some of the paddle-steamers carried it on their paddle boxes. As part of the house flag and ensign it has been flown on Manx ships at least as long as the Company itself has been in existence. Old prints survive to show it flying from the stern of vessels that may have been built even earlier.

No objection was made to the triskele (as it is called) until more than 100 years after the Company was formed. It is believed that an officer of the Royal Navy was returning to the Island on leave when he noticed the flag and reported it. No evidence has survived to substantiate this story but at a board meeting held on June 30, 1932, the flag was discussed and the following minute duly appeared:

". . . . . letters from the Government Secretary and the Attorney General that their attention has been directed by the Home Office, London, to the defacement of the Red Ensign used on this Company's steamers with the Three Legs on the fly, without official authority to do so, which constituted an offence under the Merchant Shipping Act of 1894, the penalty being £500 for each offence.

"After discussion it was agreed, on the motion of Mr. Cowley, that the embellishment complained of be removed as soon as arrangements for the supply of new bunting could be made, and that the Government Secretary and the Attorney General be informed accordingly."

There the matter rested until years later Major T. E. Brownsdon, then a Director of the Company, and now its Chairman, considered the situation unsatisfactory as every small island in the British Commonwealth seemed to have its own distinctive ensign. He obtained the permission of the Board to take up the matter with the then Government Secretary.

After a great deal of correspondence official sanction was obtained in a simple letter, dated September 10, 1971, which said: "I am writing to inform you that Her Majesty the Queen has signed a Royal Warrant granting authority for the Red Ensign flown by vessels registered in the Isle of Man to be defaced by the emblem of the Three Legs of Man."

The emblem of the island thus reappeared on its Red Ensign, and today is flown on all Manx registered vessels from car ferries to private yachts.

BUILDING COSTS.   The cost of building new ships, or occasionally purchasing secondhand ones, is listed in Chapter Three. It has been possible to trace the cost of all but seven, these mostly bought in from the market. It is unnecessary to repeat the costs in full here, but the following gives a fair summary of the spiralling capital outlay involved.

Ship   1.   *Mona's Isle*.   Built 1830. Cost £7,052.

Ship   5.   *Ben-my-Chree* (I).   Built 1845. The Company's first iron steamer. Cost £11,500.

Ship 16.   *Mona* (II).   Built 1878. The Company's first single-screw steamer. Cost £19,500.

Ship 23.   *Tynwald* (III).   Built 1891. The line's first twin-screw steamer driven by triple-expansion engines and its first building specification requiring a full electrical installation. Cost £58,683.

Ship 27.   *Viking*.   Built 1905. Triple-screw turbine. The first Steam Packet ship to be turbine driven. Cost £83,900.

Ship 45.   *Lady of Mann* (I).   Built 1930, the Company's Centenary year. Twin-screw geared turbine. The largest ship ever built for the Company. Cost £249,073.

Ship 50.   *King Orry* (IV).   Built 1946. Twin-screw geared turbine. The first ship to be built for the Company after World War II. Cost £402,095.

Ship 57.   *Manx Maid* (II).   Built 1962. The first Steam Packet ship designed as a drive on-drive off car ferry carrying 80 cars. Cost £1,087,000.

Manx Maid (II) ready to leave Liverpool on her maiden voyage, 23rd May 1962.

Ship 61. *Mona's Queen* (V). Built 1972. The first diesel passenger ship to be built for the IOMSP. Cost £2,100,000.

Ship 63. *Lady of Mann* (II). Built 1976. Very similar to the *Mona's Queen*. The fourth car ferry in the fleet. Cost £3,800,000.

The *Lady of Mann* (II) is launched at Troon.   G.E. LANGMUIR

SALARIES AND WAGES.   It is not customary for shipping companies to give full details of their wage sheets and their salary agreements. In this the Steam Packet Company is understandably no exception. All staff belong to their respective professional associations or unions. The masters are represented by the Mercantile Marine Service Association, other officers by the Merchant Navy and Airline Officers Association, and the crews by the National Union of Seamen. Workers in the shore establishments belong to their appropriate craft unions.

The salaries or wages involved are vastly different from those to be found in the early records of directors' meetings. In January, 1832, for instance, it was solemnly resolved that Captain Milligan, Master of the Company's second ship, the *Mona*, should have his salary increased from £84 to £100 a year. Eight years after that it was decided that all masters of the line's vessels should be paid £150 a year. Out of this they had to provide their own food and supply their cabin with candles, get their washing done, and defray any other personal expenses while on board.

The first report of wages in detail was tabled in February, 1845, when the renowned Captain Gill was receiving £150 a year. Chief mates, now first officers, were paid 33s. 9d. a week, second mates 25s., seamen 19s. 3d., cooks 15s., carpenters 21s., chief engineers 50s., and second engineers 30s. The minute ended with the happy item that the office boy at Douglas was paid 3s. weekly.

In another 13 years these rates had risen somewhat, but the year 1858 saw a marked decline in traffic, doubtless due to a trade recession in Lancashire. A reduction in wages was ordered and chief mates went down from 36s. 6d. to 33s. 6d. a week, seamen were docked 2s. to 20s., and coal trimmers a similar amount to 18s. At the end of the following year a new scale for captains was announced. Four categories of captains were created, and first captains went up to £300 a year with their board while on service. Second captains received £275, third £250, and fourth £225.

In this erratic expansion the office boy was not forgotten. In 1866 his wages were increased to 5s. a week and nearly two years later to 6s.

From such humble beginnings did costs mount steadily. In 1978 the Company's complex annual salaries and wages bill amounted to £2,750,000.

EVERYDAY.   The man in charge of the everyday running of the Company is Mr. S. R. Shimmin, Director and General Manager. He joined the Company in the 'thirties as a junior in the Douglas office and was a Fighter Command pilot in the R.A.F. in the Second World War. The two men who could be regarded as his principal aides on the seagoing side of the operation are the Marine Superintendent and the Superintendent Engineer. The former is Captain C. Harvey Collister, who joined the Company as a lad and became captain of a number of its ships before his shore appointment. The Superintendent Engineer is Mr. Michael Casey, who started as an apprentice in the Company, went to sea as an engineering officer for nearly 20 years, and received his present appointment in 1976.

Where the maintenance of the ships is concerned the Marine Superintendent is responsible for the decks and above, together with the hull of the ships; the Superintendent Engineer is in charge of everything below decks, together with the vessels' electrical equipment.

The Marine Superintendent has the responsibility of linking the management with the captains and officers afloat. In association with the Traffic Superintendent he works out the Company's timetables well in advance and together with the Superintendent Engineer he organises a programme for the winter overhaul work, including dry-docking arrangements. These schedules need to be arranged with the utmost care so that reserves are available to meet any emergency, and at the same time to ensure that the vessels meet the overhaul requirements of their various Department of Trade and Industry certificates.

In the winter he is aided by a Shore Captain. This is a temporary duty taken in turn by the masters from the ships that are laid up for the winter. Part of the work consists of deciding on the best course for the vessels at sea having regard to the prevailing weather in Manx waters and for this purpose the Shore Captain keeps in touch with the Meteorological Office at Ronaldsway and with the Coastguard Service. In the event of an easterly gale making berthing at Douglas inadvisable he will confer by radio with the ship's captain and if necessary, will consult with the Marine Superintendent. It may finally be agreed that the incoming ship will berth at Peel on the west side of the Island. Luckily, this decision is only

Manxman (II) arrives at Peel after being diverted from Douglas by an easterly gale.   W.S. BASNETT

necessary in winter gales blowing in at Douglas roughly from south-east to north-east, which is reasonably rare. The diversion is an expensive procedure as the Company provides transport back to Douglas for the passengers, and needs to see that mail vans, goods vehicles, shore staff, and the like are switched across the island in time for the berthing behind Peel breakwater. The ship herself incurs added costs with extra fuel consumption and staff overtime. The back-up programme has to be transferred from Douglas to Peel for the departure to Liverpool the following morning, assuming that the vessel has been unable to go round to Douglas during the night. In all, the extra cost of a Peel berthing is estimated at more than £500. In the abnormal winter of 1978-79, with its severe easterlies, ships were diverted from Douglas to Peel on 18 occasions — roughly three times the winter average.

PASSENGER TRAFFIC. The passenger traffic carried by the Steam Packet Company has varied widely over its 150 years; poor summers and good summers make the weather a vital factor in what is still primarily a holiday trade, except for freight. At the same time the British holiday itself is changing; package tours to the Mediterranean resorts have had a drastic effect on Britain's own domestic vacation trade. The Manx have made strenuous efforts to extend their season with special offerings for pensioners, and by such inducements as reduced fares.

A summary of 11 years in the 60's and 70's tells its own story.

YEAR	Total Summer Day Excursions and Charters to Isle of Man.	Total other arrivals in I.O.M.	Total arrivals in I.O.M.	Total passengers conveyed all sailings including outside Charters.
1968	97,670	274,450	372,120	799,876
1969	93,464	291,790	385,254	822,750
1970	98,132	280,072	378,204	813,733
1971	88,112	263,763	351,875	770,084
1972	109,007	261,830	370,837	780,672
1973	117,890	274,980	392,870	844,219
1974	101,242	250,288	351,530	746,570
1975	138,753	287,021	425,774	909,556
1976	133,432	281,396	414,828	872,037
1977	101,405	276,617	378,022	777,672
1978	104,100	301,280	405,380	830,609

Broken down into months these figures show a very similar yearly pattern. Here are the figures for the two years 1969 and 1978 showing the monthly incoming movements, including excursions and charter traffic, on the Company's ships.

	1969	1978
January	2,420	4,065
February	2,233	2,885
March	3,649	10,131
April	11,942	6,264
May-September	351,397	363,748
October	6,583	8,105
November	3,006	4,287
December	4,024	5,895

The swing in the March/April figures is due to the date of the Easter week-end. The monthly figures emphasise the traffic's dependance on the holiday trade, and show the mainly static peak over recent years.

An early photograph of Prince's Landing Stage at Liverpool.

It was not always so. In the 1830's the Company was averaging 20,000 passengers yearly, a figure rising to 42,389 in 1846, and 48,000 in 1851. The opening of Prince's Landing Stage at Liverpool gave the traffic a fillip from 1857, with the figures reaching 100,000 by the early 1870's. The opening of the Victoria Pier, Douglas, on July 1, 1871, produced another big traffic boost.

The traffic increased to 286,418 in 1883. At about this time there was much speculative excitement and optimism in Douglas with some of the more ambitious of the local bankers confidently predicting that there would be a million summer visitors before very long. It is doubtful if this figure was ever approached, but before the First World War the number of summer visitors certainly exceeded 600,000, nearly all of the traffic being handled by the Steam Packet Company.

In 1893 the Company carried 516,359 passengers and in 1903 the figure had increased to 711,514. In 1911 it was just short of the million and in 1913 it was 1,152,048, the summer season having been described at the time as the most successful in the island's history. In 1920 the first reasonably normal year after the 1914-1918 War, the number of passengers carried was 1,094,220. Nine years later in 1929, the figure had risen to 1,177,799. The total number of holidaymakers, of course, would have been less than half these numbers, for they are a combined tally of travellers, and not a count of individuals. Precise figures of the incoming holidaymakers are hard to come by in those years, but 634,000 — probably a record — went to the Isle of Man in 1913, and fewer than 400,000 in 1958.

PASSENGER FARES. Taken over 150 years passenger fares have obviously increased dramatically, along with costs, but the increases have been erratic. The following gives a representative summary of standard rate return fares between Douglas and Liverpool, Fleetwood, Ardrossan, Belfast, Dublin or Llandudno over nearly 80 years.

1901 — 10s.	1939 — £1 1s.
1914 — 10s. 6d.	1947 — £1 15s.
1921 — £1 2s. 6d.	1979 — £18.60

In the early days fares sometimes varied sharply according to the season of the year and competition. For the winter of 1833 the cabin fare was 15s., which included food and rowing boat hire, while steerage was half that amount with free boat hire, but no food. In April, 1835, these prices were cut and in 1838 they were reduced yet once more in mid-summer. As has been said in an earlier chapter there were even cut-throat periods when a rival line would run itself on to financial rocks, in one case charging a mere shilling a crossing.

PASSENGER TAX. The levy on passenger fares was introduced by the Manx Government in 1883 as a method of raising money for the maintenance and development of Douglas harbour. It started at a penny a fare on both departures and arrivals, but inevitably it rose steadily. By January 1, 1979, the rate had increased to 16½p. per passenger, 40 times the rate at which the tax had started.

Needless to say the Company's directors strongly resented its introduction and at their meeting on February 26, 1884, they considered the impost "Inequitable, arbitrary and unjust." Times may change; but never the dislike of taxes.

The Company now pays over £300,000 a year to the Isle of Man Harbour Board covering both passenger tax and harbour dues.

CAR FERRIES. Until 1962, when the *Manx Maid* (II) went into service as the Company's first drive on-drive off car ferrying passenger ship, there had been a steady increase in the number of vehicles carried by the Company since the Second World War. In 1961 10,561 cars were transported. With the arrival of the *Manx Maid* the traffic started a dramatic upsurge. In 1962 the increase was nearly 50 per cent over the previous year and by 1977 the trade showed an almost sevenfold increase over the 1961 figure. Again in 1978 there was a further rise in the traffic, with 77,987 vehicles being carried.

The figures for 1961-78 are as follows:

1961	10,561	
1962	15,149	*Manx Maid* in service as the Company's first car ferry.
1963	18,610	
1964	22,088	
1965	25,024	
1966	24,387	*Ben-my-Chree* in service; second car ferry.
1967	34,519	
1968	36,873	
1969	41,577	
1970	43,066	
1971	44,790	
1972	49,710	*Mona's Queen* in service; third car ferry.
1973	56,033	
1974	55,337	
1975	63,091	
1976	68,373	*Lady of Mann* in service; fourth car ferry.
1977	71,410	
1978	77,987	

The 1966 traffic, when the *Ben-my-Chree* became the second car ferry on the station, was less than it would normally have been owing to the protracted seamen's strike.

The introduction of car ferries has also seen an increase in the number of motorcycles carried, but it has only been twofold and so nothing like as spectacular as the figures for cars. The Isle of Man has a unique place in the motorcycling world, with its T.T. races in June, Grand Prix in September and rally fixtures during the summer. In 1978 there was a record number of 30,201 motorcycle arrivals by Steam Packet ships.

Before the car ferries were introduced by the Company the number of solo and combination motorcycles exceeded the numbers of cars and vans — the year 1961 being typical, when there were 15,259 cycles against 10,561 4-wheeled vehicles. These are the figures of motorcycle *arrivals* at Douglas. The sharp drop in the 1966 figure, once again, was caused by the seamen's strike.

1961	15,259	1967	15,654	1973	14,384
1962	15,620	1968	15,035	1974	19,753
1963	16,584	1969	14,997	1975	20,925
1964	14,911	1970	16,571	1976	23,548
1965	17,910	1971	16,981	1977	22,205
1966	9,571	1972	15,849	1978	30,201

ROUTES.   Douglas is now the only Manx port used by the Steam Packet Company, with the occasional exception of Peel, where ships berth for shelter from easterly gales. In May 1979 Peel was also used for schools sailings to the Island from the U.K. and the Irish Republic.

Douglas did not always have this monopoly. There were services from Peel to Belfast and from Ramsey to Whitehaven, while steamers from Douglas to both Belfast and Ardrossan would call at Ramsey in one or both directions. There is no record that the shallow harbour at Castletown has been used by the Company for passengers, but they have used it for small coastal cargo ships.

There were other services that have been discontinued. The Company no longer has regular runs from Douglas to Heysham or to Blackpool, and there was at one time a limited run from Douglas to Greenore on the northern boundary of Eire.

Before the First World War there was a service to Workington, and earlier than that one to Garliestown in southern Scotland, while Ramsey had its own direct service to Liverpool. Today the routes have been simplified. In addition to the Liverpool run there are regular summer sailings from Douglas to Fleetwood, Ardrossan, Dublin, Belfast and Llandudno.

Ben-my-Chree (IV) at Dublin in June, 1965.

King Orry (IV) at Llandudno on the opening day of the Steam Packet's Liverpool-Llandudno service, Sunday, 2nd June 1963. On Sunday, 2nd Sept., 1973 the service was operated for the first time by a car ferry (*Ben-my-Chree* (V)).   F. C. THORNLEY

A fine study of *Ben-my-Chree* (V) leaving Fleetwood in 1978. C.V. CLARK

The Douglas-Fleetwood service goes back to 1842 and continued as a seasonal service until 1961, after it had been used regularly in the emergency caused by the Second World War. In that year, however, the route was abandoned until 1971, when a new berth was used, the original landing stage having been considered to have become unsafe with age.

The link with the North Wales coast goes back to the very start of the Steam Packet Company, for the inaugural voyage of the *Mona's Isle* in 1830 was to Menai Bridge carrying the subscribers who had first made the enterprise possible. Excursions to Llandudno have been popular from the early days of the Company and in the opposite direction the route became a regular summertime run from 1961 following the withdrawal of the North Wales steamer, *St. Seiriol*. Two years later the Company took over the summer sailings from Liverpool to Llandudno operated by the Liverpool & North Wales S.S. Co. Ltd. which ceased to trade at the end of the 1962 season. These sailings are day excursions allowing passengers from Liverpool to visit the Welsh resort. The ship then takes local holidaymakers or those who have remained on board on a cruise along the Anglesey coast, calling again at Llandudno before returning to the Mersey. No vehicles are carried on any sailings to or from Llandudno.

SAILINGS AND MILEAGE. The total distance covered by the Company's fleet in twelve months is now about 160,000 miles. The traffic is at its busiest on the Friday night through Saturday and Sunday at the end of the annual T.T. week. Up to 60 passenger-carrying sailings take place during that time, returning well over 30,000 passengers, 2,000 cars and over 10,000 motorcycles to the mainland and to Ireland.

CATERING.   Catering is an important part of the operation of the Steam Packet Company. In the earliest days the captains of the individual ships were responsible for the catering and although this was hardly desirable, it was no uncommon arrangement afloat in those days. By about 1858, however, the catering side had grown to the point where it needed to be centrally organised, so the Company took it over and created a Catering Department.

The work grew steadily until in 1889 the catering side was sub-let to a well-established Douglas firm. It was generally felt that they did an excellent job, but they found it unprofitable. Victualling afloat is an intricate business, with often erratic demands on labour. The outside contracting lasted until 1960, when at the end of October the local brewery and provision firm withdrew. It could not be made to pay and the task reverted to the Company.

CARRYING THE MAIL.   The Company first carried mail in 1831, and has held a Post Office contract ever since. Inevitably the development of air services has diverted some of this traffic, which is a very important prop to the Company's operations. It was, in fact, the Post Office demand for daily mail carriage in the 1870's that triggered off the decision to run a service every weekday.

In the early days the Postmaster-General was not conspicuously generous, offering £3,000 a year for a daily service in both directions. The matter rested until 1867 when it was raised again, the Steam Packet directors, who were never afraid of an argument, pointing out that costs had risen considerably in the previous three years; in particular wages and the price of coal had gone up, and £3,000 was just not adequate.

The argument drifted on. In 1871 the Company offered to carry the mails for £4,500 a year. Five years later it reiterated its willingness to sign an agreement, but costs had again risen and the price would now be £7,200 yearly. The Post Office countered by offering £3,000 or 2s. 6d. per hundred on all items carried. Henry Bloom Noble, the Island's philanthropist and at that time the Company's chairman, said that further discussion was useless.

In 1879 the Postmaster-General reopened the whole question. He invited the Company to send a deputation to London. It went; at the time the modified service was earning only about £1,000 a year. The directors then agreed to the daily run between the main ports of Douglas and Liverpool, with no traffic on Sunday. This, of course, meant a winter service; it was a development, and a costly one, but it established the Company's complete domination of the trade, and the mail contract helped to underpin it.

With this agreement in 1879 the two-way daily service came into being, to continue with scarcely a break until today.

TAKING ON WATER.   In the earliest days many steam vessels used sea water for their boilers, but the resulting costs in maintenance were alarming. Fresh water soon became essential, not just for the benefit of passengers and crew, but for the motive power. Curiously enough, the first reference to fresh water collection in the minutes of the Steam Packet Company did not appear until April 1877, when the Douglas Water Works stated that from the following month there would be a charge of £15 per vessel for a year's regular supply to a ship's tanks and 'when it could be spared' to the boilers and for washing decks. The shipping company would be expected to supply hoses and fittings and keep the hydrants in good order.

The Company asked why the charge should be raised as it had increased steadily since 1859. The directors also asked if water could be supplied by meter and at the same time instituted enquiries to see if they could get a better deal at Liverpool.

In this they evidently failed, for while they secured a minor concession from Douglas they ended up paying the £15 a year on all but one of their ships. The matter did not end there. In 1880 the two companies were wrangling over an offer to supply water on meter, at 4s. 6d. per 1,000 gallons. In 1979 the cost was 34p. (nearly 7s.) per 1,000 gallons.

The Company has similar watering facilities available at Liverpool.

SHIPS ON CHARTER. Chartering is a business within a business. It falls into two categories — the chartering of vessels when a company is short of ships; and chartering to other lines or shore organisations when there is a surplus. The Steam Packet Company has not made protracted use of passenger ships by chartering them into its service. The paddle-steamer *La Marguerite* was chartered from the Liverpool & North Wales S.S. Co. Ltd. for three months in the summer of 1919 after the fleet had been depleted in the First World War. But most of its tonnage shortfall has been made good by purchase. After World War II the Company's fleet needs were met by new building, except for occasional sailings by the *St. Seiriol*, again of the North Wales Company.

Most of the ships chartered by the Company have been cargo vessels to relieve the Company's cargo vessels for re-fit.

Charters operated by the Company are arranged when there are vessels surplus to routine requirements and a typical year's working could include excursions to the Isle of Man from Liverpool, Workington, Holyhead, Barrow, Belfast, Stranraer, Warrenpoint and Dublin. Excursions from Douglas to Heysham and other destinations also appear in the year's shipping diary.

An up-to-date charge for chartering a ship for a day depends on the distance involved, and the port of operation, for port charges vary considerably. The charge to the client will also differ according to the day of the week as week-end wages are much higher than week-day. The number of passengers to be carried also affects the cost, as passenger tax at Douglas and other ports is payable per person. These factors can make a considerable difference. Not surprisingly charter fees are now running at anything from £4,500 to £7,500 per day.

Snaefell acting as tender for the *Ascania* on her arrival at Douglas from New York on 5th June, 1952 on the occasion of a Manx "Homecoming".

What was possibly the most unusual of the many charterings with which the Company became involved occured in 1979. A film company had decided to remake the famous story of the *Titanic* disaster, in which the Cunarder *Carpathia* was involved. The IOMSP steamer *Manxman* was brought to the Island out of dock in Liverpool in March for service to the film company.

This is a far cry from the days nearly 150 years ago when the *Mona*, the second ship in the Company's fleet, could be chartered for £20 a trip.

Charter rates could not be held at that level for very long, however. In 1846 the *Tynwald* was chartered to the Liverpool and Belfast Company at a rate of £300 per week or £200 for each voyage. In all she earned £16,749 while on charter, a useful contract that was ended on the last day of the year when she collided with the British Mail steamer *Urgent*.

CHAPTER ELEVEN: *Property & Installations*

THE APPROACH TO THE MAIN HARBOUR AREA AT Douglas is dominated by the Sea Terminal and by the head office, warehouses, subsidiary buildings and workshops of the Steam Packet Company, whose combined site could fairly be described as being abreast of the entrance to the inner harbour and opposite the head of the roads leading on to the modern Victoria and King Edward piers.

The Company has played no direct part in the gradual evolution of Douglas Harbour, except by paying its passenger taxes and harbour dues, and by the simple fact that it is the Harbour Board's main source of income.

The original harbour dates back to before 1750; it now has a few berths for small coasters, inshore fishing vessels and yachts, but dries out at low tide except for the trickle of a small river. The Isle of Man rises from a shelf, which gives it superlative fishing grounds but poor harbours; there is no deep water. Ramsey, Castletown and the inner harbour at Peel all dry out apart from their restricted stream water. Douglas, as it grew, needed to move its berths seawards.

Accordingly, about 1760 the first pier was built out to sea. It did not survive many winter storms and was replaced in 1801 by the Red Pier, which took eight years to build on the same site; it extended farther out to sea and provided a promenade for the townsfolk. Yet it was still not long enough.

By 1864 the Manx authorities had built out a pier from the southern shore on the opposite side of the Douglas water. It gave partial protection in winter storms but it stood for a mere three years.

The next pier to be built was the Victoria, driven out from the Pollock Rock, north of the Red Pier, and considerably longer. The two piers were roughly parallel and the new one had the great advantage of saving passengers a possible wetting. Steamers could now come alongside at any state of the tide and so save the traveller an ordeal by rowing boat.

The harbour continued to have its troubles. A new Battery pier was built in 1879, but it was damaged over the years by storms. In the 'thirties the King Edward Pier was built to replace the Red Pier. The Victoria Pier was lengthened and widened in 1950, and it then stretched out 3,000 feet into the sea. The next development came in 1978 when the Harbour Board erected a roadway and a link-span unit near the shore base of the Victoria Pier to facilitate the loading and unloading of drive-through car ferries.

The original offices of the Steam Packet Company were on the North Quay, between the Market Place and Parade Street. The site has since been cleared and the nearest landmark to it today would be the Douglas 'bus terminal. These modest premises were soon inadequate, however, and in the summer of 1846 the directors bought a herring curing house owned by a Mrs. Bell. It was freehold and directly opposite the discharging berth of the Company's ships.

Widening of Victoria Pier in 1950.

In order to buy it the directors borrowed £2,000 and put up £200 of their own money. They were on little risk but they had to secure the permission of the subscribers, as was the custom in those days. They said that they would be happy to keep the property themselves if the company did not want it. The subscribers, however, were wise. Mrs. Bell's building was pulled down, new offices built, and the directors congratulated the company on its wisdom in taking over the property, while the subscribers congratulated the directors in their turn. On this subject, at least, everyone was happy. The site is now part of the Company's warehouses.

In 1867 the Company bought the old Pier Inn, which it added to its warehouse and workshop area, thus expanding along the waterfront. The price paid was £1,880. The site was at the base of the Red Pier, but it was not large and is now part of the container unloading bay.

By this time the Steam Packet was actively developing its own maintenance and repair services. It had a smithy for its horses and was also doing engine-room repair work and carpentry, as the paddle-steamers of the day needed much servicing.

The Company was an important customer of Gelling's Foundry, a firm that played a considerable part in the 19th century story of Manx industry. It was established about the same time as the Steam Packet Company and had its plant on the South Quay opposite the Steam Packet premises. The firm still survives, but as a retail shop in Victoria Street; the foundry itself started to run down when the shipping company changed over to oil burners, and the old foundry was eventually sold to the Douglas Gas Company in 1968. The name of Gelling's Foundry still survives on many a man-hole cover on the Douglas streets.

The next move forward was in 1880 when the Company bought the Imperial Stables and Yard. This was at the back of the Imperial Hotel down at the Red Pier, and was a valuable addition to the warehousing area. A new smithy, engineers' shops and a brass foundry were created. This was the forerunner of the larger engineering department of today. Work was indeed starting to be moved into the Company's own premises rather than into the foundry on the other side of the quay, although the heavy castings for furnace plates and the like continued to come from Gelling's for some years.

In 1887 the Company bought the Imperial Hotel itself. This again was on the Red Pier waterfront and was soon converted to become the new head offices, with the engineering shops and the stables behind them.

At the annual general meeting of 1888 the Chairman announced that four of the company's ships were being overhauled, while the *Snaefell* (II) was having its promenade deck aft extended with a new one being built up forward. This work, he said with reasonable pride, was being carried out in Douglas from the Company's own shops by its own staff.

The alterations carried out to *Snaefell* (II) by the Company's staff are clearly shown in this photograph of her leaving Ramsey loaded with troops.

A familiar summer afternoon scene in Douglas Harbour during the fifties. L. to R. *Lady of Mann* (I), *Viking* (astern), *Victoria, King Orry* (IV), *Snaefell* (V), *Tynwald* (V) and *Mona's Isle* (V)

Two years later in 1890 the Bath Place Yard was bought, and in 1891 the annual meeting was informed that the Company was now sole owner of the land between the Old and New Piers.

During the 1880's the Steam Packet Company had been making steady and very solid progress, but it was a time of surging and erratic ambition in the Island's business world. One dubious enterprise was known to the islanders as the Bridge Company, whose object was to build a suspension bridge across Douglas Harbour not far from where the Swing Bridge was subsequently situated. The idea was nothing if not grandiose. An impressive tower, some 300 feet high, was to be built on the north side, and from near the top of it a suspension bridge was to provide a spectacular roadway to the South Quay, continuing to a Marine Drive that would be built along some of the island's finest scenery. The Tower of Amusement, as it was called in the Company's prospectus, was to have a circular base on an area directly next door to much of the Steam Packet property, fronting on Parade Street.

The tower and bridge were due to be finished in 1891, and the foundation stone was laid in October 1890, which meant that the idea was already seriously behind schedule, but the site had at least been cleared and the concern of the Steam Packet largely overcome. The enterprise was a failure, and the Douglas Head Suspension Bridge Company, as it was properly called, ran into hopeless difficulties and liquidation became inevitable in 1892.

The following year the Steam Packet Company acquired the site for £11,026. It had once been called the Hippodrome and had housed circuses. It was rebuilt to extend the warehouse area, and it meant that the Company owned nearly the whole of the considerable island site between the top end of Bath Place and the waterfront of the harbour to the south side of the Red Pier. The principal exception was the Royal Hotel which stood at the south-west corner at the harbour end of Parade Street and the Steam Packet Company duly added this to its portfolio in 1913, making the whole area some seven acres.

The Company's head office in Douglas built in 1969   W.S. BASNETT

Douglas Sea Terminal waiting hall. Band concerts given here on summer evenings are very
popular with holidaymakers.   F.C. THORNLEY

Shortly before the outbreak of the 1914-18 war the warehouses were replanned, altered and extended. The site now stretched from the Red Pier to the Victoria Pier and the Company could reasonably be said to dominate the harbour. The old Royal Hotel now houses the general offices of the Goods and Catering departments; the Harbour Board retains one small office on the waterfront next door to the office of the Goods Manager.

In 1969 the Company built its present head offices at the extreme northern end of its area. Before that, in 1946, it had bought a range of buildings in Fort Street opposite the 'bus terminal and a hundred yards or so from its main complex. These buildings today house the engineers' shops, which come under the Superintendent Engineer who has his office in the building, and the carpenters' shop which is the charge of the Marine Superintendent.

These works are on full 24 hours alert, seven days a week, and a team can be sent out to the harbour to cope with any mishap that may occur in a crowded sailing schedule. Up to 30 men, many of them seamen from the Company's ships who have transferred to shore service, work in the shops, where there is a small iron foundry and equipment for all but major engine maintenance.

CHAPTER TWELVE: *Liverpool and other Agencies*

Fᴿᴏᴍ ɪᴛs ᴇᴀʀʟɪᴇsᴛ ᴅᴀʏs ᴛʜᴇ sᴛᴇᴀᴍ ᴘᴀᴄᴋᴇᴛ
Company's link with the United Kingdom has been dominated by its main route to Liverpool
and it had its first agent there right from the start.

Mark Quayle and Son of Liverpool was a Manx firm and Mark Quayle, who died in 1833,
was the first of the Company's agents there. He was followed by James Duff, who was in turn
followed by T. D. Moore and J. Christian in January 1835. Eleven years later Moore became
sole agent. He was the son of one of the founders of the Steam Packet Company and came
from Cronkbourne on the Island.

He was not yet 40 when he died in 1851, to be succeeded by Thomas Orford, who created
the noted agency of Thomas Orford and Sons. Orford was the Company's agent for 52 years
until 1903. He was a vigorous 40 years of age when he first took the appointment; he had been
trained with John Bibby and Co. and had then worked for James Duff, becoming a ship broker
before his appointment to the Steam Packet.

A busy scene on the Mersey in the days of Thomas Orford. The Steam Packet Company's *Mona's Isle* (III) is on the left.

He was later joined by his three sons, Joseph, Thomas and William. He died in 1903 at the advanced age of 92, having taken an active interest in the affairs of his business until his last few years.

The three sons carried on the agency. Joseph, who was born in 1868, was the last survivor of the trio. It was very much a family business and Joseph's two sons, William and Thomas, joined the firm. Mr. Harold Orford, the last member of the Orford family, retired in 1970, thus ending a long and highly successful association with the Steam Packet.

He left behind him an office in India Building and staff of about twenty together with a road haulage business which was largely involved in transport work on behalf of the Steam Packet Company.

The Liverpool waterfront — famous the world over.

The Company then took over these firms, including the staff and offices. The Steam Packet also owns the Ireman Stevedoring Company, which employs about 70 dockers who man its cargo berths in the East Hornby Dock at Bootle, down river from Liverpool. The Ireman operation originally started in association with an Irish company that was bought out later. It leases a berth and cargo sheds owned by the Mersey Dock & Harbour Company and its direction also comes from the India Building office.

The director in charge of the Company's Liverpool interests, is Mr. Andrew Alexander, who is closely involved in its affairs, and is at present Deputy Chairman on the main Board in addition to his work at Liverpool. Mr. Alexander first established himself as a ship surveyor and later became a director of the Liverpool & North Wales S.S. Co. Ltd. which ran pleasure trips from Liverpool to North Wales and from Llandudno to Douglas. He joined the Steam Packet Company board in 1959, and was thus for a time a director of both companies. When Mr. Harold Orford retired he took over as the Company's Liverpool agent. The Liverpool office is by far the most important of the Steam Packet's agencies for it is the only one that handles freight. In addition, for nearly two-thirds of the year the passenger service is only from Douglas to Liverpool, the other services being purely seasonal.

A happy Steam Packet occasion on the Mersey. *Manx Maid* (II) (right) greets her new sister, *Ben-my-Chree* (V) as she leaves for Douglas on her maiden voyage on Thursday, 12th May, 1966. F.C. THORNLEY

Nevertheless the Company has had a Glasgow agent for many years, most of the time the firm of Rennie and Watson. Recently one of its principal men was Mr. Gerry McBride and when the agency was wound up in the 1960's Mr McBride became the Steam Packet Company's representative in Scotland.

Another of the Company's agents is Mr. Billie Stephens of Belfast, who had joined his father's firm of W. E. Williames and Co. when they were the Steam Packet's agents before the war. Mr. Stephens then took over at the end of the Second World War and has represented the Company in Ulster to the present day. He had a most remarkable war, being one of the very few prisoners of war who escaped from the notorious Colditz. He made his way towards Switzerland and slipped over the border to the neutral country. There he was helped by a young woman who became his wife and is now living in Belfast.

In Dublin the Company is represented by the British and Irish Line and in Fleetwood the port manager for the British Transport Docks Board, Mr. David Dixon, looks after the Company's interests as part of his general work. Llandudno sends thousands of day tourists to the Isle of Man every summer and the business is substantial. The agent there is Mr. Gerry Bouwman, who is a full time Steam Packet employee. He looks after the Llandudno operation in the season and for the rest of the year works from the Liverpool office.

CHAPTER THIRTEEN: *Finance and the Future*

In 149 YEARS THE STEAM PACKET COMPANY moved forward from an opening subscription which gave it a capital of £7,250 to an authorised capital of £3,000,000. In that time its annual turnover increased from a few thousand pounds to something in excess of £10,000,000. Its progress was at times erratic. Its success depended heavily on a sense of service to an island public, and there were years when the Manx suffered from the effects of hardships that had started on the mainland. On such occasions the Company suffered too.

It was and has remained a highly specialised business, for which it has had spasmodic need for large sums of money, more than it could generate from its immediate cash flow. Shipping companies have been ever thus. It also evolved something of a dual nationality in its ownership, which explains why for a number of years it held some of its directors' meetings in the north of England. Further it must be one of the few prosperous concerns that has ever met to decide whether to take the cash and close itself down, or simply carry on.

At first all was plain steaming in the Company's history. Two hundred and ninety shares of £25 paid for the *Mona's Isle* in 1830 and set the business on the move. A further subscription of 190 shares a year later provided for the *Mona*. Working expenditure was defrayed from working income. In 1833 the Company had a cash balance of £604 and paid its subscribers a dividend of 5 per cent. The following year the capital was increased from £12,000 to £24,325 represented by 973 shares. The enterprise was moving rapidly, and a formal Deed of Association was drawn up in 1838. In 1841 it was decided to create half shares in the Company at £12 10s. each. This was for the building of *King Orry* (I). The idea was that half shares would then be issued for a total value of £6,000, and pay half the cost of the new vessel. The other half was to come out of income, which was rising satisfactorily. The stockholders were duly offered the new half shares with a right to dispose of the allotment if they did not wish to hold it. The method was successful.

It was repeated in 1845 on a one for one rights issue basis for the building of the *Ben-my-Chree* (I) and by the following year the subscription capital had risen to £40,688. This was done by increasing the number of half shares and then making an allotment of quarter shares of £6 5s. each.

In 1845 there occurred another example of the shareholders overruling the directors in the handling of the Company's affairs. This time there was no argument, as years earlier there had been over the temporary dismissal of Captain Gill, but on October 23 the Board had the curious task of writing to Robert Napier and telling him that they had been limited by the subscribers in the price of a new ship; so they asked him to produce the best vessel he could for £21,000. The result was *Tynwald* (I).

These sums were substantial matters in 1846, when the directors had to inform the subscribers that little more than half the latest issue of new shares had been taken up. Indeed, the Board succeeded in rescinding a resolution that a dividend of 5 per cent per year should be paid, as they felt that the whole of the Company's earnings should be applied to payment of the new steamer.

In 1847 the dividend was passed and it was not until 1850 that the Company reverted to the 5 per cent that the subscribers had come to expect. Then during the next ten years dividends were occasionally waived as money was wanted for instalment payments on new vessels.

Yet although they could be hard in some matters the Company's management and subscribers could be generous on occasion. Trade was bad in Lancashire in the early 1860's owing to the depressed condition of the cotton industry, and in 1862 the Company voted the then appreciable sum of £500 towards the relief of distressed cotton operatives.

By 1864 the capital structure had risen to £66,046, and by 1882 to £80,734, being rounded up the following year to £82,500. By then various commercial enterprises on the Isle of Man had been closely studying the Companies Act of 1865 in the United Kingdom, that had led to the introduction of the limited liability company. The Steam Packet considered the question for some time but in 1875 it was decided to delay taking action.

The 1870's were mainly a progressive time in the Company's history and in 1878 the dividend was increased and a bonus added. Steamer captains were given higher salaries and their pay when their vessels were laid up was increased to two-thirds of their full rate instead of one half as before.

In 1880 the Company held its 50th annual general meeting and the report lamented another downturn. The "continued depression of trade, and the unprecedented severe weather of the past season, particularly during the months of July and August, have caused a decrease in the gross earnings of £4,554 7s. 9d. being chiefly occasioned by falling off in passenger traffic."

The great debate about the assumption of limited liability was concluded in February, 1885, when a resolution proposed from the Chair by H. B. Noble was carried unanimously.

The fleet is at full stretch only during the summer months and winter lay-up has always been a heavy expense. Here *Victoria* (left) and *Manx Maid* (I) are laid up in Douglas Harbour in September 1949.

No vessel in the Company's fleet gave better service than *Fenella* (I). Her lifespan of close on half a century was not without incident, however, as on 9th Sept. 1884 she went aground at Menai Bridge (above).

Below she is seen at Liverpool Landing Stage in 1926 towards the end of her long life. In contrast her sister ship *Peveril* (I), seen here at Ramsey (facing page), was lost in a collision in 1889 when only fifteen years old.

The Company was duly registered as a company limited by shares under the Companies Acts of 1865 to 1884. The following year the capital was increased to £100,000. Within the next five years 100,000 more shares were issued, this time of £1 each. The total capital was thus £200,000 made up of varying denominations.

As the century neared its end the Company had not only put itself on a new legal footing, but it had brought its workaday practice more up-to-date. Its old minute books suggest that it had always been closely supervised by its directors in its everyday running. Indeed for many years they seemed to be excessively concerned with detail and they had always submitted their tentative major decisions to their subscribers for approval. Now, as the Company grew in size, so the work of the directors became more that of decision-making, requiring only formal approval of shareholders at the annual meeting.

In 1910 the shares, half shares and quarter shares that gave the Company a complex stock structure were all converted into £1 shares, and have so remained ever since. At the outbreak of war in 1914 it had a capital of £200,000 in £1 shares and had part issued an authorised £150,000 in debentures.

One of the most extraordinary episodes in the history of the Company occurred at the annual general meeting at the end of February, 1919. The position then was that the Company, plainly under-capitalised at £200,000, had more than £700,000 in investments behind it, and the remains of a fleet that had been written down to under £70,000; these two items were in addition to assets in buildings, plant, stores and the like, of the sort that would be expected of a shipping company. Four ships, including the cherished *Ben-my-Chree* (III) had been lost in the war, and from chartering fees, compensation payments and awards from underwriters, the Company had received more than £500,000, which formed the bulk of its investment portfolio.

The problem was a simple one. Resources although formidable were quite inadequate to make up the lost tonnage by ordering new shipping. Costs had risen as a result of the war. It was soon widely known that there was a basic disagreement among the directors. One section argued that the Company could be wound up if the shareholders so wished and £5 could be distributed for every £1 of the issued capital.

At the annual general meeting a group of shareholders did in fact propose that the directors should either offer to sell the undertaking to the Manx Government or dispose of the operation as a going concern. The meeting spilled over from one day to the next with an extraordinary general meeting sandwiched in between. A record number of shareholders attended, the 700 mainland shareholders being strongly represented. The Chairman, Dalrymple Maitland, who was at the time the Speaker of the House of Keys, led a strong counter-attack proposing that the Company should carry on and continue its service to the Island. In the various votes one director, identified with the £5 for £1 movement, failed to be re-elected, and there was even a move to call for the resignation of another although he was saved by the intervention of the Chair. It was an acrimonious affray.

Another group proposed that the capital should be increased by a bonus issue of two shares for one, bringing the authorised capital to £600,000 in £1 shares. This would bring it more into line with the Company's assets and was agreed by a substantial majority. The Chairman's call for local patriotism and for a sense of service had carried the day. The continuity was preserved.

It is not unknown for expansionist shipping companies to be under-capitalised. The Company's capital was increased yet again in 1954 by a bonus issue of three for two, bringing it up to £1,500,000.

This move coincided with an upsurge of interest in the Company. Rumours had been circulating for some time that a take-over bid was being hatched, the name of Michael Jay emerging as the mysterious bidder. He was unknown on the Island, but on November 26, 1953 he met the Board and said that he represented a group, whose constitution he would not divulge, and that he intended to make an offer of £3 a share for the £1 shares. Jay, who was visiting the Isle of Man for the first time, outlined his ideas, but the Directors were unimpressed. They considered that he knew nothing of the special difficulties concerning the Manx shipping operation, and such ideas as he put forward were regarded as positively bad. He promised to submit his proposals to the next full board meeting but nothing was heard from him by that date.

He did, however, write a week later and ask for information regarding the current financial position. He was told he must wait for the annual report which would be sent out in February, and the Board made it clear that they would not recommend his offer to shareholders. There was every sign that a fight was in the offing.

The matter was left for the annual general meeting, at which it was expected that Jay would be present. A Douglas cinema was booked to hold the number of shareholders expected to attend. In all this excitement the shares had risen from about two pounds each to more than three, but the bid never seriously materialised.

The shareholders had meanwhile received a letter from the Company Secretary saying that all possible steps would be taken to ensure that the equity would represent a sound investment. The general reserves would be capitalised to provide the share bonus.

The directors of the Isle of Man Steam Packet Co. Ltd. photographed at the inspection of the *Manx Maid* in Manchester Dry Dock, April 1979. Back row, L. to R.: K. C. Cowley. W. A. Gilbey, J. E. K. Rae, S. R. Shimmin. Front row, L. to R.: A. Alexander, J.P. (Deputy Chairman), T. E. Brownsdon, O.B.E., J.P. (Chairman), F. C. Kissack, F.C.A.

The meeting promised to be a major occasion. In fact it turned out to be something of an anti-climax. Jay did not turn up and he had already sold almost all his holding. He may have been interested in a fleet of ships that were worth substantially more than the figure at which they stood in the Company's books. When he realised that they were not to be picked up his enthusiasm for the Manx shipping world evaporated.

There was another stir of financial excitement in the early 1970's. It became known that the Slater Walker group was picking up shares in the Steam Packet Company, eventually building up a total holding of rather more than six per cent of the equity. The Manx Government was advised; they too started collecting shares and accumulated a holding that matched Slater Walker and thus would help to fight any possible takeover bid. It was confirmed, however, that the shares were being acquired as a solid investment with a high yield for a unit trust and that there was no suggestion that the Slater Walker people were attempting any takeover. There was no cause for concern. There was still less when the main Slater Walker company ran into liquidity problems. The unit trust holding was purchased on behalf of the Manx Government, bringing its holding in a company vital to the Manx economy up 13.8 per cent.

The capital increase that had been agreed at the time of the Jay affair remained until February, 1979, when the Company increased its authorised capital to £3,000,000 and capitalised £750,000 from its general reserves by allotting a one for two bonus issue to shareholders; this brought the issued capital to £2,250,000. In 1978 there had been a profit of £1,135,628 against £439,000 in the previous year. With such a profit an increase from a modest capital of £1,500,000 was plainly justified.

So much for the past, stretching successfully over 150 years during which the world economy has gone through boom and depression, recession and expansion, war and peace. Throughout it all the affairs of the off-shore Isle of Man have run roughly in parallel with its larger neighbour.

Meanwhile the Steam Packet Company has played its role as the vital lifeline and has prospered, at times while facing severe competition. Its policy has always been one of cautious and steady progress. During its history it has kept in close touch with all marine developments as they have arisen — the conveyance of passengers from the early days, the handling of cargo and later of vehicles, and aids to navigation and marine engineering in general.

When the Company has satisfied itself that some innovation suits the specialised pattern of its business and is financially viable, it has adopted it. A modern example of this was the new design of the *Manx Maid* (II), which went into service in 1962 as the first drive on/drive off car ferry on the Irish Sea. Until then cars for shipment from the mainland to the Isle of Man had had to be craned aboard. The Steam Packet was quick to develop the unitization of cargo traffic on the Manx trade.

"cars . . . . had to be craned aboard."
The Fort Anne Hotel — a landmark for nearly 200 years — was demolished in 1979.

The Company realised back in 1973 that the service may need to accommodate lorries approaching the juggernaut size and its interest was then notified to the Isle of Man Harbour Board.

On the Steam Packet's side it was realised that as and when finances and circumstances permitted it was desirable to extend its service to include large commercial vehicles of a size and height that could not be accommodated on its car ferries. These ships offer full facilities for private cars and medium sized vans, but the decks give insufficient headroom for

In the 1979 Douglas Carnival parade this giant model paddle steamer, built by the Steam Packet Company, won first prize. A worth-while exercise in public relations.

the larger type of vehicle. The Company's forward planning estimated that the service should be extended to the ro-ro type of ship in the early 1980's when at least one of its existing vessels would be due for replacement.

The matter came up for discussion with the Harbour Board early in 1977. In furtherance of the Company's policy the internationally known firm of consultant engineers — Burness, Corlett and Partners — were engaged to examine the practicality of installing a linkspan unit that would enable tall and heavy vehicles to drive straight on and off in the shallow and very exposed Douglas Harbour, where, as we have seen, berthing can be exceedingly difficult in certain weather conditions.

The positioning of such a linkspan and anchorage is only one of the many problems involved. A suitable site for the mainland terminal of such a service has also to be found and developed or adapted. This alone could be a costly matter. However, the Company is advanced in its preliminary planning. The building of a favoured linkspan design also involves a very considerable capital outlay, not made any easier by the nature of the home harbour. Then there is the obvious problem of the first ship or ships to specialise in this sort of traffic. It is probable, however, that appropriate vessels of the right tonnage could be found in the used ship market, where owners have changed to a policy of using larger tonnages and have smaller ships for disposal. So if preliminary negotiations are eventually completed the shipping side of the development need cause no exceptional holdup.

By September 1979 the full report from the consultant engineers had been received, and the Company has been able to consider the development more deeply. Although no firm decisions could be expected at so early a stage, the first moves were taken to proceed with discussions with the Isle of Man Harbour Board, who control the Harbour area on behalf of the Isle of Man Government.

In this way, piece by piece, like an advance on a chess board, the future is planned from the successful experiences of the past.

A sketch by John Nicholson of the Company's Centenary Steamer, *Lady of Mann*. Her spacious decks, well-appointed lounges and seaworthiness endeared her to the Island's holidaymakers during the thirties and in the years following the Second World War.

Acknowledgements

Many people and sources have helped the writer in compiling this book. When its Chairman, Major T. E. Brownsdon, first decided to allow me access to the Steam Packet Company's files both he and Mr. Sydney R. Shimmin, General Manager and a Director, gave freely of their time and advice.

Thanks must go also to Mr. Michael Casey, the Company's Superintendent Engineer, who gave up a number of week-ends to comb through the sometimes conflicting records of the early ships, checking them as far as possible with his own department's marine records.

Captain C. Harvey Collister, Marine Superintendent, also lent material and gave helpful advice. Other executives who helped include the Goods Manager, Mr. Norman Lea, and Catering Manager, Mr. Tom Lynch. Mr. Melvin Barcroft of the central administration helped in arranging the examinations of the Company's earliest minute books, of which he has special knowledge.

Mr. Louis Bridson is a typical example of a Steam Packet man who has compiled material about the Company's ships ever since his boyhood. He has a remarkable collection of files, including detailed copies of all relevent entries in the Register of the Registrar General of Shipping and Seamen. Particular thanks are due to him for the loan of this highly valuable source material.

Material was also given to me by Commander Harold H. Thornber, R.N.R., of Blackburn, who has studied the early development of naval aviation warfare, in which Steam Packet ships played an adventurous and successful part in the First World War.

Special thanks are due to the Manx Museum's Director, Mr. A. Marshall Cubbon, and to the ever helpful Miss Ann Harrison, its Archivist and Librarian.

From London the Ministry of Defence, particularly the Naval Historical Branch, was especially helpful in providing photocopies of important log cards and detailed notes of various Manx ships on wartime service.

Miss Anna C. Urband of the Information Division of the U.S. Department of the Navy, Washington, D.C., provided a copy of the official history of the *Gettysburg*, which had once been the IOMSP paddler *Douglas*.

Mr. F. B. O'Friel kindly gave details of German records that disposed of the theory that the *Fenella* was salved at Dunkirk and subsequently served in Russia.

The Glasgow Museum of Transport also helped in providing details of early material on shipbuilding for the Company.

Thanks are also due to Mr. J. G. Bell, who was for many years manager of the Company's Ramsey office; to Mr. Percy Coupe of Douglas, who has collected a mass of material on the activities of his native town, and to Mr. J. H. Kerruish, of Maughold, a veteran of Operation Ariel in the Second World War.

A number of retired Masters of Steam Packet vessels helped me with reminiscences that added detail to outlines of Second World War operations which had been supplied to me by the Ministry of Defence. I am indebted to Captain Thomas Corkill, who retired as Marine Superintendent, and who lives in Onchan; to Captain John E. Quirk, Chief Officer of the *Fenella* at Dunkirk, who retired as Commodore and now lives in Port Erin; Captain Westby Kissack, of Douglas; Captain (and later Commodore) Lyndhurst Callow, of Douglas; Captain Ernest McMeiken, who also became Commodore, now living at Onchan and Captain Frank Griffin, of Port Erin, who retired as Marine Superintendent.

Mr. J. Stowell Kenyon provided me with extracts from his taped conversations with that remarkable woman, the late Miss Janet Gibb, They were made at the Grove, Ramsey, where she lived to a great age in her elegant old home, which she bequeathed to the Manx Museum. Her recollections of the *Ellan Vannin* disaster, the official inquiry, and the loss to the Island's life, were recorded when she was 95, and they tallied closely with the Company's records.

I am indebted to Mr. A. M. Goodwyn for his admirable drawing of the first *King Orry*'s Napier engines. It was based on an old print that was unsuitable for reproduction.

Two men made a very special contribution to the book. Mr. W. S. Basnett's photographic work needs no commendation from me. He is a fine marine photographer who concentrates on transport subjects. In addition to his camera work he was of great help in searching for and identifying long-forgotten pictures of early ships, several of which appear here for the first time in a modern book.

Secondly, I feel the rare obligation as the author to acknowledge the great help of Mr. Leslie Stephenson, a director of the publishers, who at my request, agreed to edit the book. His firm, which was established in Prescot in 1761, are specialists in the publication of works on shipping and he himself has a considerable knowledge of the history of Isle of Man Steam Packet vessels. This partly arises from his interest in transport and shipping generally, but is added to by the fact that he and his family, who live in Port Erin, have for years been Steam Packet contract holders. This has given him an affection for the Steam Packet vessels and their personnel that is typical of their regular passengers.

A number of publications contain valuable source material; the earliest book to give prominence to the subject was John Kennedy's *The History of Steam Navigation*, published in Liverpool in 1903. This is a valuable reference work and devotes a whole chapter to the Steam Packet Company. The following year A. W. Moore, who was respected as a local historian and was Speaker of the House of Keys and a director of the Company, wrote *Historical Account of the Isle of Man Steam Packet Company Limited*. This was the main source of the contents of the Company's Centenary book, published by them in Douglas in 1930, and largely written by Philip W. Caine. These two books are now collectors' items at auctions of Manx books. So is a booklet giving an account of the Company's ships in the First World War, written by C. J. Blackburn, who was the Company's Superintendent Engineer.

On wider subjects there are three valuable sources of modern Manx history with a bearing on the Steam Packet Company. Two of them are papers: *The Story of Douglas Harbour*, by J. C. Brown, is in the *Proceedings of the Isle of Man Natural History and Archeological Society*, Vol. 5, Number 4, and is very well-researched history of the harbour development; *Douglas Head Suspension Bridge*, by F. K. Pearson, is in Vol. 7, No. 85 of the *Journal of the Manx Museum*, 1969. The third, by the late W. T. Lambden, is *Air Services*, a highly detailed history of the growth of civil aviation in the Island, published by the Omnibus Society, London, in 1965 in their *Manx Transport Systems*. Details of these three short works can be obtained by inquiry at the Manx Museum, Douglas.

The subject is covered in one modern book, *Ships of the IOMSP* by Fred Henry, revised by Mr. F. B. O'Friel (Brown, Son and Ferguson, Ltd., Glasgow) and first published in 1962; small and convenient, it is well-packed with a useful record of the Company's long list of ships, and is particularly strong on the history of its routes. The Steam Packet Company is also given pride of place in *West Coast Steamers* by C. L. D. Duckworth and G. E. Langmuir (T. Stephenson and Sons Ltd., Prescot, Merseyside). This book, now out of print, covers the history of steamers and ferries that have worked the coastal and passenger trades in ports from Liverpool and the north-west down to Bristol, and in all it gives details of approximately 800 vessels.

Lastly, I should like to express my thanks to Mr. John Nicholson of Leeds who designed and executed the attractive dust cover. He is also responsible for the frontispiece, which originally appeared on the cover of the April, 1978, issue of *Ships Monthly* whose publishers, Waterway Productions Ltd., of Burton-on-Trent not only gave permission for the picture to appear but also kindly loaned the colour separations.

Many others have helped in various ways and to them all I record my grateful thanks.

C. C.

Mona's Isle (I)

Douglas (I)

Mona (II)

Ben-my-Chree (III)

Lady of Mann